ACCESSIBLE
HOUSING
BY DESIGN

ACCESSIBLE HOUSING BY DESIGN

Universal Design Principles in Practice

STEVEN WINTER ASSOCIATES

McGraw-Hill

New York   San Francisco   Washington, D.C.   Auckland   Bogotá
Caracas   Lisbon   London   Madrid   Mexico City   Milan
Montreal   New Delhi   San Juan   Singapore
Sydney   Tokyo   Toronto

Library of Congress Cataloging–in–Publication Data

Accessible housing by design : universal design principles in practice
  / Steven Winter Associates.
       p.   cm.
   ISBN 0-07-071174-7
   1. Dwellings—Access for the physically handicapped—United
States.   I. Steven Winter Associates.
   NA2545. P45A33   1997
   720′ .87′ 0973—dc21   97-6579
                                                                CIP

McGraw-Hill

A Division of The McGraw·Hill Companies

1 2 3 4 5 6 7 8 9 0   1IMP/1IMP   9 0 2 1 0 9 8 7

ISBN 0-07-071174-7

Printed in Hong Kong through Print Vision, Portland, Oregon.

Steven Winter Associates, Inc. staff members who were instrumental in the development and production of this document include:

Alexander Grinnell
Principal-in-charge

Peter A. Stratton
Project Manager

Editorial
Cynthia J. Gardstein
Michael J. Crosbie, Ph.D., AIA
Adrian Tuluca
John Amatruda

U.S. Department of Housing and Urban Development Office of Policy Development and Research

Alan J. Rothman
Project Manager

McGraw-Hill staff:

Wendy Lochner
Sponsoring Editor

Jane Palmieri
Editing Supervisor

Pamela Pelton
Production Supervisor

Design
Andrew P. Kner
Art Director

Michele L. Trombley
Assistant Art Director

Elizabeth Rosen
Symbols

Mary Jo Peterson, CKD, CBD, CHE
Kitchen and Bathroom Consultant

Cover Photo
©1995, John Caleb Schwartz

FOREWORD

As we become aware of the growing need for environments that are usable by all persons, increasing numbers of Americans are accepting the principle that accessibility in all types of housing makes good sense.

The term "Universal Design" has come to symbolize those features that make housing usable to persons with a broad range of needs. This publication, *Accessible Housing by Design: Universal Design Principles in Practice,* showcases 16 projects from many parts of the United States that illustrate these principles. The projects represent well-designed, marketable and generally affordable examples of Universal Design in recently completed or proposed single-family housing.

I am pleased to present this useful publication in the hope that the reader will find it thought provoking and a valuable resource, and that it will lead to a greater understanding and implementation of Universal Design concepts.

Michael A. Stegman
Assistant Secretary for Policy Development and Research
U.S. Department of Housing and Urban Development

INTRODUCTION

Our increasing awareness of America's large aging population, our acknowledgment of the needs of persons with disabilities and the fact that, as individuals, our own physical and mental abilities will inevitably change has alerted many of us to the need for more accessible (barrier-free) working and living environments. This awareness led to the Fair Housing Amendment Act of 1988 and the Americans with Disabilities Act of 1990. While the provisions of these acts do not apply to privately owned single-family homes, they have created general interest in Universal Design principles. Recognition of this interest prompted this book. These principles call for buildings and outdoor spaces to be "universally" designed, useable by a broad range of human beings including children, older people and those of differing stature and abilities.

The purpose of this book is to showcase recent projects by builders, architects and designers that illustrate successful Universal Design concepts as applied to single-family housing. These case-study projects vary greatly in responding to different programmatic, design and user requirements. Some represent recently built houses, some are remodelled structures, while others are works in progress. There are a few homes that are luxurious, but most are quite modest. This diversity is intentional. What these projects have in common is that they successfully, and in most cases seamlessly, integrate Universal Design features within the standard design elements of the house, often with modest or no additional cost. All of the designs are intended to blend in unobtrusively with neighboring structures.

The design features that make them accessible simply represent good design decisions that are intended to support and enhance the occupant's lifestyle so that they can remain and function well in their familiar surroundings throughout their lives. Because the elderly represent one of the largest and fastest growing segments of the population, the market demand for Universal Design features will continue to expand.

As an aid in illustrating Universal Design features, a series of symbols has been created that accompany the drawings and photographs and highlight these features. A list of these symbols and the features is found on page 9.

TABLE OF CONTENTS

METHODOLOGY

Prior to the selection process, the U.S. Department of Housing and Urban Development and Steven Winter Associates, Inc. developed a list of Universal Design criteria in order to evaluate individual projects. A "call-for-entries" was placed in various national trade publications and entered on Adaptive Environments' World Wide Web Site. Numerous other resources were investigated for qualifying projects including: universities with programs in Universal Design, organizations that promote or conduct conferences on Universal Design issues, associations or councils that represent people with disabilities, older individuals and consumers of Universal Design products, industry professionals with expertise in Universal Design and accessibility, professional organizations that represent architects and designers, and manufacturers of accessible products and assistive devices.

Candidates were contacted and asked to submit their projects for review. Each project was evaluated against the selection criteria, and the most interesting and successful projects were chosen for publication.

SYMBOLS

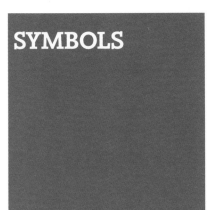

BASIC ACCESSIBILITY FEATURES

- Step-free accessway
- Level, protected entrance
- Low-threshold at entry with 36-inch-wide minimum door width
- No level changes on entrance level
- Motorized stair lifts and elevators
- At least one bedroom and an accessible bathroom on the entrance level
- 32-inch-wide minimum clear door openings
- Lever hardware on doors
- Minimum 36-inch-wide, short hallways
- At least one bathroom that provides sufficient clear floor space for wheelchair access to all fixtures
- Grab bars or bathroom walls reinforced for future installation of grab bars
- Reinforced ceiling for installation of a powered track lift
- Kitchen plan that provides easy access to and use of all elements

SECURITY OR COMMUNICATION SYSTEMS

- Audio/visual alarms
- Programmable lighting
- Motion detectors
- Electric door locks
- Occupancy sensors
- Exterior door sidelights
- Intercoms

EASILY TRAVERSED FLOORS

- Low-pile carpet
- Slip-resistant floor coatings

REMOTE CONTROL FEATURES

- Fireplace
- Windows
- Door openers
- Lighting
- Television and/or stereo

ACCESSIBLE LAVATORIES, SINKS, AND COUNTERS

- Open kneespace below sinks, cooktops or counters
- Removable or slide-in base-cabinet doors
- Removable base cabinets
- Insulated or protected pipes to prevent scalding

ACCESSIBLE BATHING

- Roll-in shower
- Shower seats
- Bathtub deck doubles as a transfer surface

VARIABLE HEIGHT COUNTERS

- Multi-level counter heights
- Adjustable counter heights

ACCESSIBLE WORK SURFACES

- Roll-out carts
- Pull-out trays

HEARING IMPAIRMENT AIDS

- Smoke/burglar alarms trigger blinking lights
- Doorbell triggers blinking lights
- Ringing telephone triggers blinking lights

VISUAL IMPAIRMENT AIDS

- Tactile surface cues
- Illuminated work surfaces
- Contrasting floor borders provide room dimension cues
- Contrasting banded edges along countertops provide cues to counter locations
- Countertop surface borders provide counterspace cues
- Strategic use of contrasting colors
- Voice activated home communication/security systems

9

SCHULTZ RESIDENCE

Architect
Corson Associates, Architects
Sebastopol, California

This renovation is for a client with lower body paralysis. Responding to the need for a barrier-free environment, the architects provided a skillful blend of structure, open planning, large glass openings, skylit areas and Universal Design features.

The entire central area of the house was rebuilt, the main entrance moved, and the garage expanded. Access from the street is achieved with a bermed walk. The removal of interior walls opens direct physical and visual paths through the core of the house. A large central skylight is located above the new post-and-beam structure. Two-level kitchen counters, each with a sink, provide work space for the entire family.

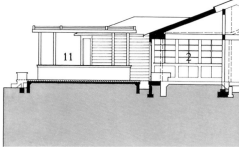

Section A-A

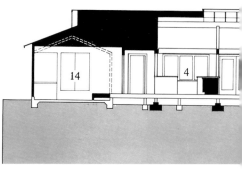

Section B-B

The effort to reduce interior obstacles required the removal of many walls, most of which were located in several small, dark rooms. As a result, a new roof structure was devised as a means of providing a separate architectural identity to the spatially integrated kitchen, dining room, living room and family room. The new purlin-and-beam roof structure is supported by columns located at the corners of the different spaces. The resulting open plan with its defined central axis allows travel between the spaces with limited turning movements. The central skylight creates a large interior pool of light.

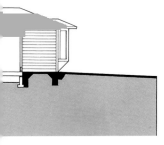

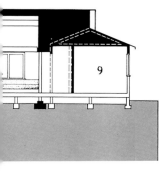

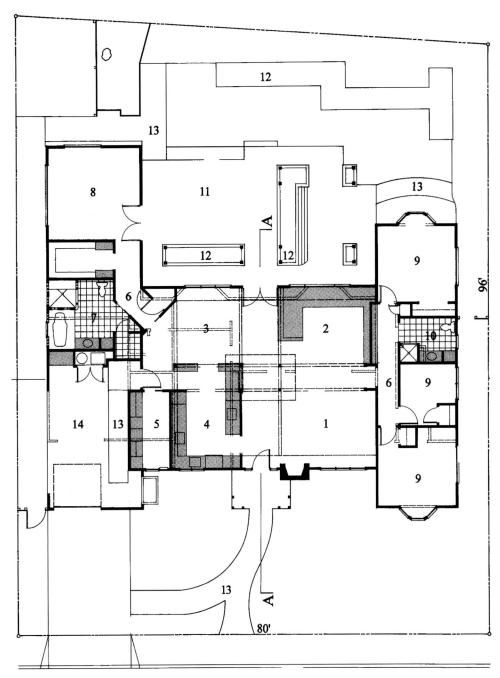

1. Living room
2. Family room
3. Dining room
4. Kitchen
5. Laundry
6. Hall
7. Master bathroom
8. Master bedroom
9. Bedroom
10. Bathroom
11. Terrace
12. Raised garden
13. Ramp
14. Garage

Floor plan and sections of the accessible renovation

In the original house, the front porch and steps were inaccessible. In the remodeling, the front door opens directly across a $\frac{1}{2}$-inch-high threshold to a large front porch. From the porch, a brick path connects to both the front public sidewalk and the driveway. The new landscape treatment effectively integrates the ramp by berming gently up to its sides.

The winding path that connects the front entry to the street

Raised planting boxes were built in the rear yard before the renovation of the house began. The client requested a terrace that would provide additional accessible planting boxes and an operable shade system. This was accomplished by continuing the beam and column theme from the main entry of the living area to the outdoors. Above this structure is a cable-supported fabric shade that the client can adjust as needed. The new, raised planting boxes are accessible from all sides. A new walk built around the side of the house provides a direct, level connection between the rear yard and the front of the house.

Accessible terrace with raised planting boxes and an operable shading system

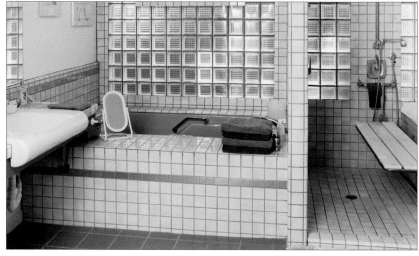

The family room

The client requested a family room that would allow her to leave her wheelchair and sit with family members. The wide window seat/sofa, separated from the dining room by a cabinet, serves this purpose. The bookcase was designed to contain accessible electronic equipment.

Master bathroom

The bathroom was designed to be light, airy and accessible. This was accomplished by using glass block panels at the exterior wall and between the tub and shower. The shower, with a low curb to contain water, has a folding seat that extends beyond it. This allows the client to leave her wheelchair outside the curb and transfer to the shower seat from the dry floor. The seat slides back and folds out of the way of other users.

Accessible laundry area

The washer and dryer have front-mounted controls and side-hinged, fully-opening doors. They are installed so that the drum is at lap height. Work surfaces are found above and beside these machines. A fold-down ironing board is provided.

Accessible kitchen

Central to the design of the accessible kitchen was the desire to have bi-level counter space large enough to accommodate more than one person at a time. This was accomplished by making the side of the kitchen with the cooktop and oven accessible at the lower level. Included on this side are an accessible corner sink and pull-out table drawers that provide an additional horizontal surface next to the stove. The oven has a side-hinged door and is sufficiently high, allowing wheelchair access under the pull-out surface. The refrigerator door swings 180 degrees against the adjacent pull-out storage wall, allowing full access to the interior. The upper level of the kitchen has a sink and a disposal. The cabinet doors below the sink are mounted on hardware that allow the doors to open and slide back, making the sink accessible. A 6-inch-deep raised shelf at the back of the 2-foot-deep main counters provides additional storage space. Behind the corner sink, a pair of windows with low sills allows easily operated ventilation and a clear view of the street and front walk.

UNIVERSAL HOME

Architect
James Fahy Design
Rochester, New York
Builder
Whitney East, Inc.
Rochester, New York

This popular, fully accessible two-story house, built in Rochester, New York, as a model home for the local 1995 Homearama, responds to a growing regional market for accessible housing. The floor plan was designed to attract a wide market range, from empty-nesters to young couples with or without children. The animated façade blends with the local architectural context and the design skillfully integrates the accessible features inconspicuously. Constructing this home was a first-time venture for the builder, who had previously developed accessible commercial properties.

The house is approached via a gently sloping walkway from the garage to the front door. The front porch adds visual interest and provides a protective transition to the interior. Inside, double-height spaces and the open plan provide drama and ease of movement.

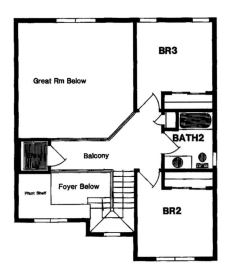

BR3

Great Rm Below

BATH2

Balcony

Plant Shelf

Foyer Below

BR2

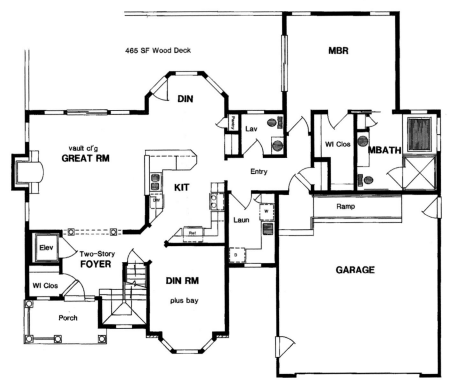

465 SF Wood Deck

MBR

DIN

vault cl'g
GREAT RM

Pantry

Lav

WI Clos

MBATH

Entry

KIT

DW

Ramp

Laun

W

Ref

Elev

Two-Story
FOYER

D

WI Clos

DIN RM

plus bay

GARAGE

Porch

Accessible first and second floor plans

The compact plan is organized around a two-story foyer with both stair and elevator access to the second floor. Ease of movement is achieved throughout with the open plan, which reduces the number of "corners" while providing space for entertaining and family activities.

The large two-car garage is van-accessible and has a ramp into the home. A laundry room is sized to provide full wheelchair maneuverability. Kneespace under the counter allows laundry sorting and folding to be accomplished from either a sitting or standing position.

The second floor contains two additional bedrooms and an accessible bath. The balcony provides views to the great room and foyer. A second-level loft space above the foyer is an option.

The rear view shows the accessible deck, ramped to grade. The home is designed with large windows positioned to maximize daylighting, which add to the overall sense of openness. Access to the deck is through low-threshold sliding-glass doors. Low windows allow full views from sitting or reclining positions.

The front porch provides shelter and a transition from the exterior to the interior. A low-threshold entry is provided at the front door, which has a sidelight to allow viewing of visitors. A security system with keypad controls is also provided.

Street view of the Universal Home, above

Rear view showing the accessible deck with ramped access to the surrounding property, below

Master bathroom. An appearance panel below the sink is provided to hide plumbing and to protect from scalding.

The master bath features a large roll-in, curbless shower equipped with a hand-held shower head and anti-scald valves. Kneespace is provided under the vanity for wheelchair access. Mirrors are installed lower than usual and all faucet controls are lever-type. There is blocking behind the drywall for future installation of grab bars.

Living area of the Universal Home featuring French doors that open onto the accessible deck.

Large windows offer unobstructed views, complementing the feeling of openness. Low-threshold double doors provide access to the rear deck. The flooring is slip resistant. The high ceiling allows for large transom windows.

Barrier-free kitchen layout

Counter height is lower than the standard 36 inches to aid accessibility. Among the many Universal Design features are front controls on the cooktop, sink-base and cooktop-base doors that slide in to provide kneespace, higher-than-standard toe clearance, and a double oven high and low. Kneespace next to the oven facilitates cooking from a wheelchair. A counter-top microwave oven is also available. The adjacent counter is convenient for loading and unloading the microwave. Roll-out shelves and pull-out storage bins are provided throughout the kitchen so that cooking activities can be performed within comfortable reach. The flooring is slip resistant.

FIELDCREST II

Designer
Miles Homes Services, Inc.
Minneapolis, Minnesota
Builder
The Philip Stephen Companies
Minneapolis, Minnesota/
Greenville, South Carolina

Miles Homes Services, Inc., the nation's 29th largest homebuilder and the largest supplier of home-building kits to the do-it-yourself owner-built and owner-contracted market, has developed a line of accessible home plans that it calls the Lifespan Collection℠. The Fieldcrest II is an excellent example of one of their in-house designed affordable and accessible plans. Models in the Lifespan Collection℠ range between 1,500 and 2,000 square feet, and are available as a complete construction package in 44 states across the nation. Universal Design strategies and products have been incorporated into each model in the collection. Many options are offered to tailor each home to the owner's specific needs, material preferences and local climate.

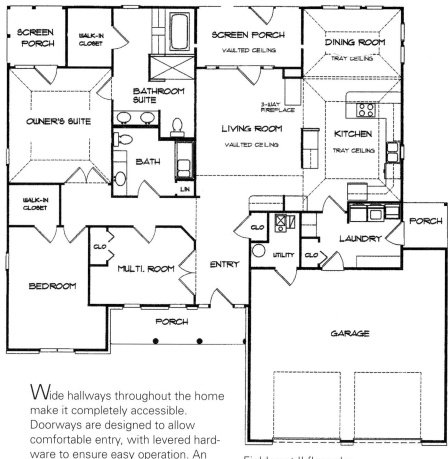

Wide hallways throughout the home make it completely accessible. Doorways are designed to allow comfortable entry, with levered hardware to ensure easy operation. An automated whole-house security system is provided. The custom kitchen offers ample space for work and maneuvering, a variety of counter heights and handy access to the laundry area and garage. Vans easily fit through the 9-foot-high garage doors. The owner's bedroom suite has an attached, fully accessible private bath suite and a spacious closet and dressing room. Additional features include low window sills in bedrooms and a second accessible bathroom.

Fieldcrest II floor plan

Front elevation

The entry features a ramp and barrier-free access over a low-profile threshold. A large porch serves as an attractive transition area and a protected waiting zone. Full sidelights at the entry door allow people of varying age or height to view visitors.

Rear elevation

Skylights ensure an abundance of light in the screened porches for year-round use. Gently sloping walks define the patio area and provide a transition to outdoor entertainment spaces.

An open floor plan allows comfortable living in well-defined spaces without visual or mobility restrictions. Wear-resistant, low-maintenance laminate wood floors permit easy maneuvering and care. Access to and from the outdoors is increased by using doors with lever handles and low-profile thresholds. The dining room has motorized windows. A remote-controlled, three-way fireplace can be enjoyed from the kitchen, living room and dining area.

Open floor plan of the Fieldcrest II

Activities in the kitchen are enhanced through accessible features such as varied height cabinets and higher-than-standard toe clearance space. Counters, work spaces and appliances can be reached from either a sitting or standing position. Both the roll-under cooktop and kitchen sink can be outfitted with automatic height-adjustment controls. The levered faucet has a pull-out spout for easy use and the kitchen window is equipped with a motorized opener. All appliances have front-panel controls.

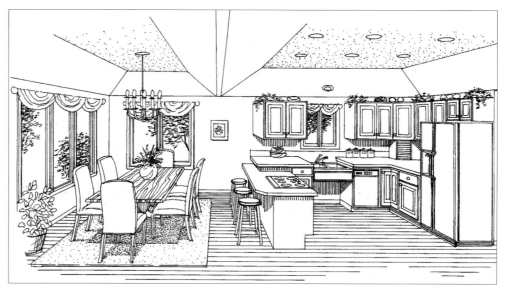

Kitchen and dining areas of the Fieldcrest II

Laundry area

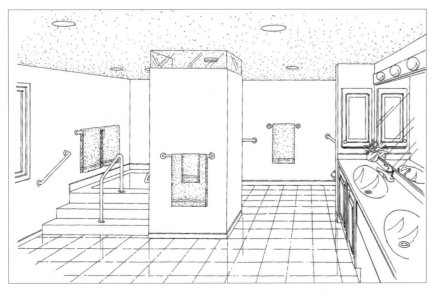

Master bathroom

Large toggle electric switches and levered hardware on entry and closet doors are included. Laundry tasks are made easier by the roll-under ironing board and front-load washer/dryer. Higher-than-standard toe clearance space facilitates wheelchair approach.

Each bathroom is equipped with a barrier-free roll-under vanity and levered pull-out sink faucets. A roll-in shower with a levered hand-held shower head on a slide bar has been selected in the master bath. The second bathroom incorporates such features as a built-in folding grab bar, automatic removable seat lift and hand-held faucet. Grab bars and toilets can be specified in varying heights.

Second accessible bathroom

23

INDEPENDENT LIVING HOMES™

Contractor
Storn Construction
Atlantic Beach, Florida

This home has become a model for accessibility in North Florida. Storn Construction, which builds exclusively for people with disabilities, has a wealth of experience implementing Universal Design concepts. The target market are individuals adding on to their homes to accommodate an aging parent, those down-sizing their homes for retirement, and older people who want to adapt their homes for independent living. The home's design is the result of a careful and thorough planning process (including measuring the occupants' height, reach, strength and mobility), and includes all the necessities and amenities to help an individual with a disability to live a full and comfortable life.

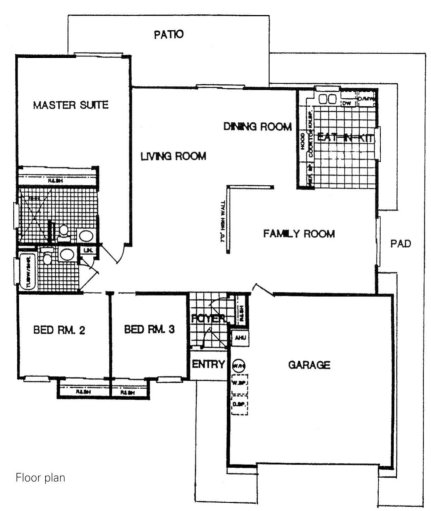

Floor plan

The open yet compact plan, with a minimum of corners, allows virtually unrestricted movement. All interior doors, both swing and pocket, are 36 inches wide. The sliding glass door in the living room has a recessed threshold and is power operated.

A control panel is located in the master bedroom to operate front and rear exterior lights, bedroom lights, ceiling fan and alarm. The large master bathroom is equipped with a roll-in shower with offset shower controls. A 5-foot-diameter clear space in front of the vanity and toilet area provides space for wheelchair maneuvering.

In the garage, maneuvering space is provided around vehicles. A level threshold at the interior door is protected by pop-up door weatherstripping. The washer and dryer are recessed into the floor several inches so that the appliances can easily be used by someone in either a sitting or standing position. The main house electrical panel is easily reachable at 43 inches above the floor.

Pop-up weatherstripping

Front elevation

Windows are placed low to allow full views and emergency egress. A side viewing panel at the front door makes it easy to identify visitors. A no-threshold front door aids access, while the entry ramp eliminates steps. Exterior water faucets are 20 inches above the ground for easy access, and exterior flood lights can be controlled from the master bedroom. All walkways, patios, porches, driveway and garage floor slope for positive drainage. A 9-foot-high garage door is provided to allow van access.

The base cabinet doors at the sink and cooktop can remain open or can be removed entirely to allow access space for a wheelchair user. Pipes beneath the sink have been moved to the side and insulated to protect users from scalding. Controls for the range are on the side within easy reach. The control switch for the range exhaust is conveniently placed at counter level. All low cabinets have roll-out shelves and the corner "Lazy Susan" aids accessibility. Additional lighting assists those with impaired vision.

Kneespace under sink and cooktop is concealled by base cabinet doors

Wheelchair accessible cooktop

The ceiling above the bathtub is blocked to accept a motorized lift

This view of the unfinished bathroom shows blocking in the ceiling for installation of a motorized lift, if necessary. Also visible is the 3/4 inch plywood surrounding the tub enclosure, which allows installation of horizontal and/or vertical grab bars in virtually any location.

THE OWENS

Designer/Builder
Design One
Lemont, Illinois

This two-story urban home, designed and built with the expressed purpose of showcasing Universal Design features, has won many awards including the 1995 Homebuilders Association of Greater Chicago (HBAGC) Gold Key. The home has an attractive street façade, a well designed and efficient plan, plus many Universal Design features that occupants will find user-friendly, all at a moderate price.

The urban-style plan of the Owens

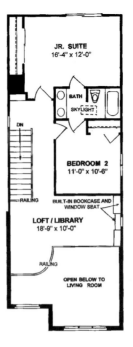

The first floor is completely accessible. The side entry conveniently opens into the kitchen area. The open living/dining area provides ample wheelchair maneuverability. All interior doors are 36-inches wide. The master bedroom bath is wheelchair accessible. The second floor can be used by a live-in assistant.

Façade of the Owens

This façade illustrates the home's urban character. A gently sloping ramp along the side of the house provides access to the side entry and connects to the rear garden. The exterior is low-maintenance brick.

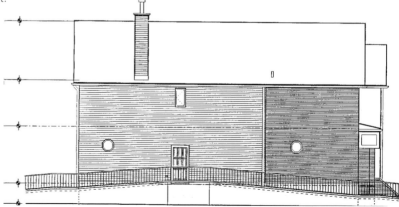

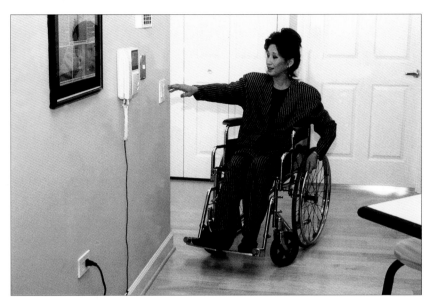

Controls for the video-entry security system and zoned home-security system are conveniently located near the side and front entry. Illuminated rocker switches and electrical outlets are placed within easy reach. Ample turnaround space is provided.

Side entry foyer leading into the kitchen area

The 7-inch risers and 11-inch treads are designed to be easily negotiated by elderly users or by people who have difficulty climbing stairs.

Easy-climb stairs

Casement windows are easy to operate with a single lever device at the sill.

Casement window locking lever

29

The kitchen sink and counters are installed at a lower than typical height with clear space underneath for wheelchair accessibility. Storage cabinets with roll-out shelving allow improved access to people with limited range of motion.

The open kitchen plan of the Owens, above

Wheelchair accessible cooktop with front controls, below

Appliances were specified for accessibility. The cooktop is lower than standard and has front-mounted control; a side-opening oven, also at countertop height, is easy to use from sitting or standing positions. A side-by-side refrigerator puts both freezer and refrigerator within easy reach.

Five critical elements are incorporated into the bathrooms: clearance below the sinks, raised toilets, lever hardware, grab bars, and slip-resistant flooring. In addition, a roll-in shower with a hand-held, adjustable shower head increases accessibility and ease of use.

Accessible bathroom, above

Accessible shower, below

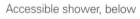

UNIVERSAL DESIGN

Designer
Shirley Confino Interiors
Norfolk, Virginia

This Universal courtyard home was introduced at the Tidewater Builders Association Homearama (a regional home show) in 1990, where it drew much attention because of its accessible design features. Universal Design elements of this home include large bathrooms, accessible storage space, easily manipulated fixtures, tactile and visual cues and a security system that can be programmed for many needs. The site surrounding the home was graded to eliminate the need for ramps.

The plan shows the unique features of this home, including the central patio design that gives the home its open and light-filled character.

The oversized garage can easily accommodate a van. All hallways are wide for easy maneuverability. The design allows for the separation of the bedroom suite from children's and guest rooms. Wide doors, elimination of thresholds, low cabinetry, tactile and audible cues, slip-resistant surfaces, task lighting, reinforced walls, backup power and security systems are all features that allow the residents to move freely about their home and to remain independent.

The electrical receptacles, controls and switches are installed within easy reach. A strobe light and audible alarm are installed near the front door to alert the occupants to fire, telephone or doorbell.

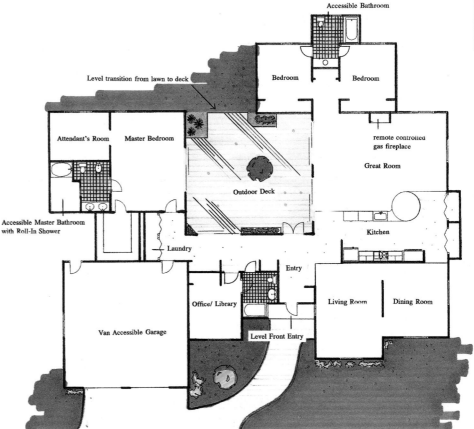

Open floor plan

The sloped pathway to the entry connects to the driveway, eliminating the need for steps. An overhang at the front entry provides shelter. Windows are installed 24 inches above the floor to allow for viewing from a seated position and for easy egress in an emergency. Windows are casement type with easily operated hardware at sill level.

Exterior view

33

The great room

The doors on the sink base are removable for wheelchair access

In the kitchen/dining and living areas abundant natural light spills into the large open family room through sliding doors that make the interior courtyard fully accessible. When these doors are open to the interior courtyard, the space for entertaining is doubled. A remote-controlled gas fireplace can serve as backup heating.

Carpets were selected for ease of maintenance and wheelchair maneuverability. The living area carpet has a level loop texture, with a double-stick underpad that eliminates rippling and provides flooring on which a wheelchair can easily roll.

Considerable attention was paid to the height of workspaces and appliances. The basic counter height is 36 inches with pull-out counters at both 28 inches and 30 inches. The double ovens were installed with the lower unit 13 inches above the floor. The pressure-activated digital controls are at 48 inches. Front controls for the range and a vent hood are placed at counter height. The built-in microwave oven is also at counter height. A pull-out drawer for storage of dishes was installed next to the dishwasher. The sink is 6 1/2 inches deep with an offset drain, allowing the plumbing under the sink to be recessed. If accessibility to the range and sink is required, the cabinets can easily be removed and replaced with panels that cover the piping.

All counter edges have an indented strip in a contrasting color as a visual and tactile cue. The base cabinet toe spaces are 8-inches high to facilitate wheelchair approach. Cabinet hardware is easy to grip. Storage for pots and pans, small appliances, and groceries is provided in two shallow closets on the side wall. Each has full-height bi-fold doors for easy access.

Accessible bathroom

The house has three accessible bathrooms; pictured above is the master bath. Handrails, low mirrors, accessible sinks, slip-resistant tiles, panic buttons and outwardly swinging doors are included. The bath suite has a whirlpool tub and a large roll-in shower. The shower contains a duplicate set of controls near the entrance for an assistant to operate. All water controls are levered and scald-proof. Two textures are used in the floor tiles to give location cues to the visually impaired. Walls are reinforced for the easy installation of grab bars at any location.

Interior court accessible from several rooms in the home

The center courtyard is accessible to the great room, hallway bedroom and bathroom, and encourages cross ventilation throughout the home. The courtyard also provides privacy and can be enclosed if desired. Plants were chosen to attract birds and provide for a variety of scents.

THE FUTURE HOME

Contractor
Valley Contractors Inc.
Phoenix, Maryland

Before

Remodeling this home for accessibility posed a unique challenge for the contractor. The 135-year-old building, originally designed as a tavern, is on a 26-acre site in Gunpowder State Park, Maryland, and is listed in the state's Inventory of Historic Sites. Therefore, it was necessary to follow the Federal Historic Guidelines while incorporating accessible features.

The exterior of the home, restored to its original appearance, is an excellent example of the area's 19th century vernacular architecture. The goal of the interior restoration was to create a "living laboratory" that responds to the needs of people with vision, hearing, speech and ambulatory impairments, creating a showcase of accessible technology. Additionally, it has been designed to study and develop solutions for those with progressive impairments.

The Future Home incorporates many Universal Design features without compromising the building's historic integrity, and is an excellent example of the use of technology to enhance independent living.

After

Before

The entry path to the home was reconfigured and now allows for a straight, level walk from the adjacent parking area. The spacious, covered porch is finished with a slip-resistant coating. Entry is through "no-threshold" sliding glass doors. Entrance features include a remote-controlled combination lock, a video camera that enables residents to see visitors, a doorbell activated in all rooms with sound and/or flashing signals, and an intercom system that allows for conversation with visitors before entry.

After

The new addition contains the front entry, foyer, dining room and living room. Floor surfaces here and elsewhere are either slip-resistant quarry tiles or low-pile carpets. Automatic lighting has been provided throughout the home. Motion sensors automatically turn lights on when human movement is sensed, and off when no movement is detected. Light switches are specified as large rocker panels, installed at accessible height. Windows can be operated manually or by remote control. Electronically controlled HVAC dampers allow for independent room climate control. The staircase features

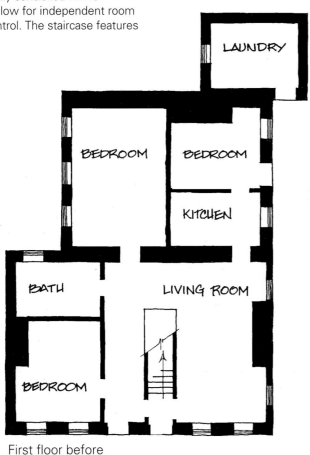

First floor before

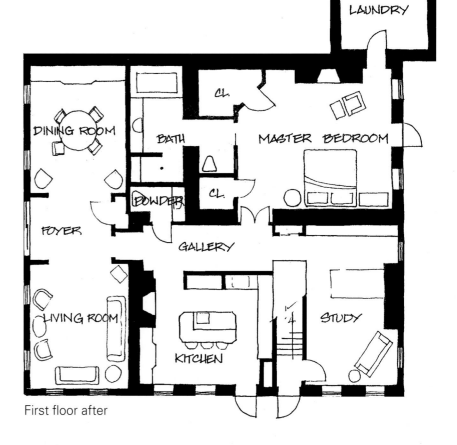

First floor after

a platform lift that can transport a wheelchair, making the second floor accessible. With two accessible bathrooms, the upstairs can be used as living quarters for a personal care assistant or for a shared housing arrangement. A swing-open motorized door is at the bottom of the stairs.

Second floor before

Second floor after

Windows are set low, enhancing the view out. The large table in the middle of the room is adjustable to either dining or coffee table height by remote control. This feature allows the dining room to serve as a media room. The entertainment unit has higher-than-standard toe space to allow wheelchair users to get close for media equipment operation.

This space doubles as a dining or media room, above

Master bedroom, below

Easy access is provided to the master bedroom through double doors placed off the 4-foot-wide gallery. A generous door allows for roll-in use of the closet. The laundry room is conveniently located off the bedroom. Technological features include a key panel that allows the user bedside access to all security systems, and a hands-free phone that enables the user to auto dial or answer by remote control. In addition, full spectrum lighting is specified for those with Seasonal Affected Disorders.

Kitchen area, above

Accessible bathroom, below

Multi-level work surfaces enable full use of the kitchen from a wheelchair or standing position. Motorized features such as vertically adjustable cabinet shelves and cooktop aid in accessibility, as does a mechanical device that horizontally moves cabinet shelves closer to the user. All appliances have Braille identification and the kitchen telephone is equipped with hearing-aid compatible features. The ceiling fan is operated by remote control. A video camera enables remote monitoring of the front entry. An exterior door makes it easier to bring in supplies and food and provides emergency egress.

The first-floor bathroom is entered from the bedroom though a wide pocket door. Grab bars placed around the room are fully functional and are a decorative feature. The shower is equipped with two hand-held shower heads and push-button plumbing controls. The vanity is completely accessible and includes conveniently located electrical outlets.

FAIRLAND MANOR

Architect
American City Building
Columbia, Maryland
Builder
Korth Companies, Inc.
Gaithersburg, Maryland

Fairland Manor is the first town home condominium community in the greater Washington, D.C. area designed to be completely barrier-free and wheelchair-accessible. The builder/developer will make any modifications, or find and install any equipment available, to meet the unique needs of the purchaser. The sales representative is trained to identify technologies and equipment in consultation with physical therapists that will permit purchasers to remain in their own homes for life.

An extensive list of options is available to customize the town home to meet the specific accessibility needs of the purchaser.

Façade of the Barclay and the Ashley

Common features of both the Barclay (left) and the Ashley (right) models are level front entry, curb cuts from parking to entry, a low maintenance brick exterior and a covered entry. A unique feature is the heated sidewalk to melt snow and ice.

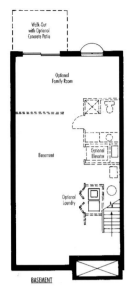

BASEMENT

Floor plan of the Barclay

FIRST LEVEL

SECOND LEVEL

Barclay labels: Walk-Out with Optional Concrete Patio, Optional Family Room, Basement, Optional Elevator, Optional Laundry, Optional Deck, Master Bedroom, W.I.C., Bath, Gourmet Kitchen, Optional Elevator, Dining Room, Living Room, Foyer, Porch, Roof, Bedroom #2, Bath, W.I.C., Optional Elevator, Den, Open to Living Room, Bedroom #3

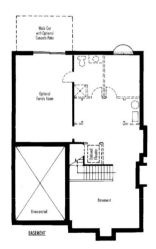

BASEMENT

Floor plan of the Ashley

FIRST LEVEL

SECOND LEVEL

Ashley labels: Walk-Out with Optional Concrete Patio, Optional Family Room, Basement, Optional Elevator, Unexcavated, Optional Deck, Master Bedroom, Bath, Gourmet Kitchen, W.I.C., Optional Elevator, Dining Room, Opt. Ramp, Foyer, Oversized Garage 14', Living Room, Roof, Bedroom #2, Bath, Den, Optional Elevator, Bedroom #3, Bookshelves, Open to Living Room

Two basic floor plans are available—the Barclay and the Ashley. Each plan is straightforward, with plenty of clear floor space for ample wheelchair maneuvering.

The Barclay is a three-bedroom home with an optional finished basement. The first level includes a master bedroom with a fully accessible bath with a roll-in shower. All windows are casement type. Motorized window and door openers are an option. The second level has a fully accessible bathroom, two bedrooms and a den.

The Ashley is also a three-bedroom unit. It includes a garage large enough to accommodate a van equipped with a lift. Ample room is provided in which to negotiate a wheelchair around the parked vehicle. As does the Barclay, the Ashley features a fully accessible bath on each level. A roll-in shower is available on the second level as an option, but is included in the standard plan on the first level. An optional elevator or stair lift provide access to the second level.

43

Accessible kitchen layout of both the Barclay and the Ashley

Living area of the Ashley

The kitchen layout is roughly equivalent in both models. Standard features in the kitchen are a side-by-side refrigerator with an ice dispenser, accessible hardware on cabinets, and clear floor area in front of all appliances. The range has front panel controls (including a switch for the disposal) and kneespace is provided under the sink. Kneespace under the counter area next to the range allows this surface to double as a work space or a dining bar. Touchless faucets are optional, as are movable cupboards and counters.

Standard features in the Ashley living room include switches at lower-than-standard height, higher-than-standard electric outlets and large, low windows for full views from a seated position. Options include a remote-controlled gas fireplace, remote-controlled motorized window openers and remote locking devices. Windows are also available with rain sensors that automatically close windows.

Second level bedroom of the Ashley

This roomy third bedroom includes low casement windows with easy-to-operate crank handles, open storage shelves for easy accessibility, lower closet rods and shelves, easy-to-reach electric switches and outlets, and low-pile carpet throughout. Available options include occupancy sensors that automatically turn lights on or off as people enter or exit the room.

Occupancy sensor

Accessible master bathroom

 This master bathroom is equipped with a roll-in shower as a standard feature. Shower controls are offset so that the water flow can be adjusted before entering. A hand-held shower head is adjustable for ease of use. Grab bars are installed around the entire shower enclosure, and a seat is provided.

Stair lift

The elevator option

An elevator shaft is included in both models. If the purchaser chooses not to install an elevator, the shaft is finished as a closet on each level. Specifying temporary closets is possible if the owner intends to install an elevator at a later time. A telephone is provided for emergency use. A stair lift is an option.

THE HERITAGE RETIREMENT COMMUNITIES

Architect
Richardson, Nagy, Martin
Newport Beach, California
Builder
US Home Corporation
Englewood, Colorado

As evidence of the increasing interest in Universal Design concepts among large home builders, US Home Corporation (one of the top five home builders in 1995) is redesigning two of its new projects, Heritage Highlands in Tucson, Arizona, and Heritage Palms in Indio, California, with accessibility in mind.

The Heritage retirement communities are high-end, single-story homes on golf courses, targeted to active adult retirees. The builder, believing that accessibility not only represents good design but also contributes to an upscale custom-built look, plans to develop options that allow homeowners to customize residences to reflect their specific circumstances and abilities.

As the preliminary designs indicate, the Heritage communities will include numerous standard and optional Universal Design features. The open

living, dining and kitchen areas provide generous space for wheelchair maneuvering and flexibility in furniture layout. Level accessways and low thresholds allow unobstructed entry. Interior doors 36-inches wide are optional. Nine-foot-high garage doors permit van access. All electrical outlets will be located at a minimum of 18 inches above the floor with light switches at 42 inches above the floor. Thermostats will be placed at easy-to-read locations.

The kitchen can include features such as varied counter heights, raised dishwashers and roll-out shelves in lower cabinets. Glass doors on upper cabinets provide a view of what is stored. A side-by-side refrigerator provides access to both the refrigerator and the freezer from a seated or standing position. Single lever faucets and faucets with lever handles

Plan 1

Plan 2

accommodate those who have difficulty grasping. Optional higher-than-standard toe clearance improves access and increases clear floor area.

Bathroom options in the Heritage communities will include roll-in showers that allow independent bathing activities for wheelchair users, shower

seats for people with difficulty standing during bathing, and bathtubs that have an easy transfer surface for people to sit before they enter the tub. Higher-than-standard toilets are also available as an option. Bathroom walls are reinforced for future installation of grab bars.

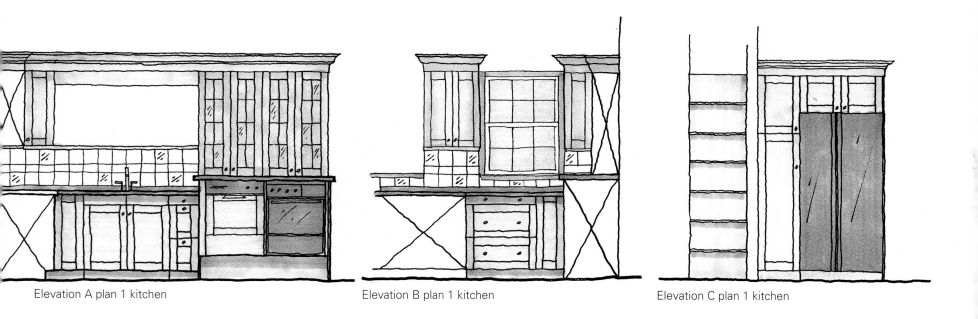

Elevation A plan 1 kitchen

Elevation B plan 1 kitchen

Elevation C plan 1 kitchen

Plan 1

Universal Design kitchen features include:

- Pantry with roll-out shelves
- Side-by-side refrigerator
- Cooktop with front-mounted controls
- Slide-in doors below sink and cooktop provide kneespace
- Raised dishwasher

- Raised oven with adjacent counter space for the placement of hot items
- Wall cabinets above raised dishwasher and oven extend to counter height and provide accessible storage

49

Plan 2 kitchen perspective

Plan 2

Universal Design kitchen features include:

- Pantry to the left of the refrigerator includes a door-mounted step stool for safe access to top cabinet
- Roll-out cart
- Pull-out trays at accessible heights
- Microwave mounted below wall cabinet is at accessible height
- Slip-resistant flooring
- Side-by-side refrigerator
- Cooktop with front-mounted controls
- Sink with single lever control
- Kneespace below sink and cooktop
- Raised dishwasher increases buffet surface and provides better access to dishwasher
- Raised oven with adjacent counter for placement of hot items
- Island provides small but functional work/storage area

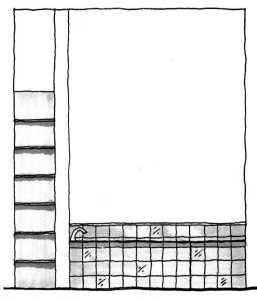

Elevation A plan 1 master bathroom

Elevation B plan 1 master bathroom

Plan 1

Universal Design master bathroom features include:

- 36-inch-wide entrance
- Split vanity allows for variations in height of user, provides a parallel approach for a seated user. Kneespace is provided below the lower sink
- Built-in deck on bathtub creates a transfer surface
- Clear floor space beyond the bath tub control wall allows a person in a wheelchair access to controls
- Open shelf storage
- Optional raised-height toilet

Plan 2 master bathroom bathtub and shower perspective

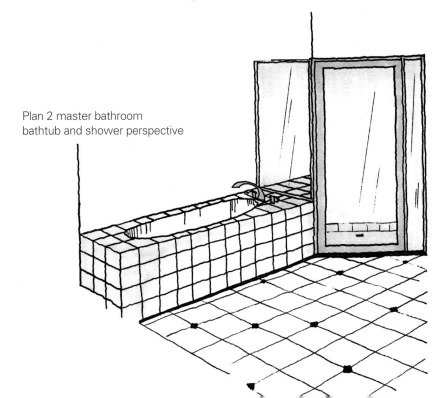

Plan 2

Universal Design master bathroom features include:

- 36-inch-wide entrance
- Built-in deck on bathtub provides transfer surface
- Pedestal sinks and wall-hung cabinetry
- Bathtub deck extends into shower and creates a shower seat
- 36-inch-wide door into shower
- Open shelves

UNIVERSAL HOME SERIES:
THE TIMBER RIDGE
T-RANCH
THE UNIVERSAL RANCH

Manufacturer
Excel Homes, Inc.
Liverpool, Pennsylvania

The Universal Home Series is a line of modular homes developed as a joint venture between Excel Homes, Inc., a large Pennsylvania modular manufacturer, and the Center for Accessible Housing (CAH) at North Carolina State University, a leading design and research center with a long-time involvement with Universal Design and accessibility issues. The Universal Home Series specifically addresses the changing needs and abilities of all family members.

The Timber Ridge T-Ranch design was developed by The Home Store of Whatley, Massachusetts, with CAH. The Universal Ranch design was submitted by Custom Care Homes, Holland, Pennsylvania. It was developed by Excel and CAH. Both homes are available through Excel Homes, Inc.

Two examples of modular homes available as part of the Universal Home Series

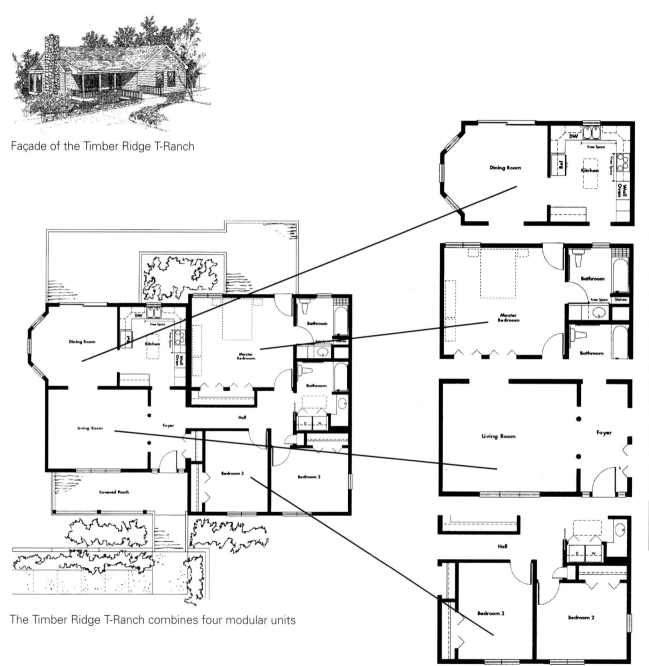

Façade of the Timber Ridge T-Ranch

The Timber Ridge T-Ranch combines four modular units

The Timber Ridge T-Ranch combines four modular units to achieve a barrier-free layout. Incorporated into the design are standard Universal Design features plus a variety of options. The level entry approach provides easy access to the covered porch that includes a parcel shelf. Sidelights and a low door threshold are provided for access and security. Other standard features include lever lock-sets for exterior swing doors, and an audible/visible smoke alarm and doorbell. An accessible rear deck and garden area connect the interior with the exterior for viewing pleasure and access to outdoor activities.

53

The open plan of the Timber Ridge T-Ranch adds furniture flexibility, provides plenty of play space for children and allows easy maneuvering for wheelchair users. A wide bay window provides interest. Large windows, approximately 18 inches above the floor, allow for full views from a seated position. Remote motorized window operation is an available option. The recessed lighting on either side of the remotely operated gas fireplace is controlled by a rocker switch easily reached by everyone including children and wheelchair users. Easy-care, slip-resistant floor surfaces, such as low-pile carpeting and vinyl flooring, are good surfaces for toddlers and allow safe maneuvering for individuals who may use walking aids.

Living/dining open plan

In the kitchen of the Timber Ridge T-Ranch, variable counter heights, pull-out shelves and convenient storage allow the entire family to participate in meal preparation. Wheelchair-accessible counters make it possible to prepare food while seated, rendering the kitchen safer and more comfortable to use. Drawers can be equipped with full extension hardware and easy-to-grip loop handles. A convenient option is the specially designed sink and cooktop section. Easy removal of the base cabinets creates kneespace under the counter. These counter heights can be set at 30 to 36 inches.

Accessible kitchen

The floor plan of the Universal Ranch has many similarities to the plan of the Timber Ridge T-Ranch: an accessible entryway, covered porch for protection, security and lighting control, and flush or low-rise thresholds are among their features. Careful site work and house placement are required to create the no-step, level approach to the entry. Circulation through the home is through open areas or amply sized hallways. The kitchen is designed to enable several people to work without getting in each other's way. Both the bedroom bath and the second bath are fully accessible. Electrical receptacles, switches, and controls are placed at easy-to-reach heights. Additional electrical outlets have been placed in the bedrooms for assistive devices. Ceilings in bedrooms and baths can support optional motorized lifts.

The Universal Ranch

The kitchen design of the Universal Ranch addresses the needs of accessibility with the following elements: loop handles, full extension drawers, storage with pull-out racks, side-by-side refrigerator, adjustable height sink and cooktop counters, front-mounted controls on the cooktop, light and exhaust fan controls mounted at counter height, kneespace with protection panel, pull-out shelf for transfer of food to and from the oven, wall-mounted oven with a wire rack at pull-out shelf height, ample clear floor space, storage on utility closet doors, and an eat-in counter with kneespace.

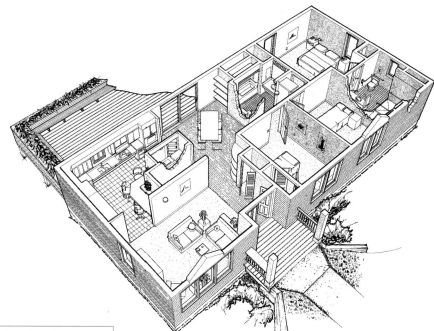

Cutaway view of the Universal Ranch

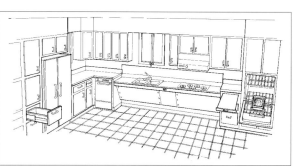

Typical kitchen

The bathroom options offered by the Universal Home Series are designed to allow a variety of bathing features: a standard tub with a fold-up seat, a tub with a transfer surface, a whirlpool tub, a 3-foot-square transfer shower and a 5-foot-square roll-in shower. Offset controls make it easy to turn on bath water and regulate temperature from outside the tub or shower. Base cabinets under the lavatory can also be easily adapted to provide kneespace. The bathroom walls are reinforced so that grab bars can be easily and inexpensively added.

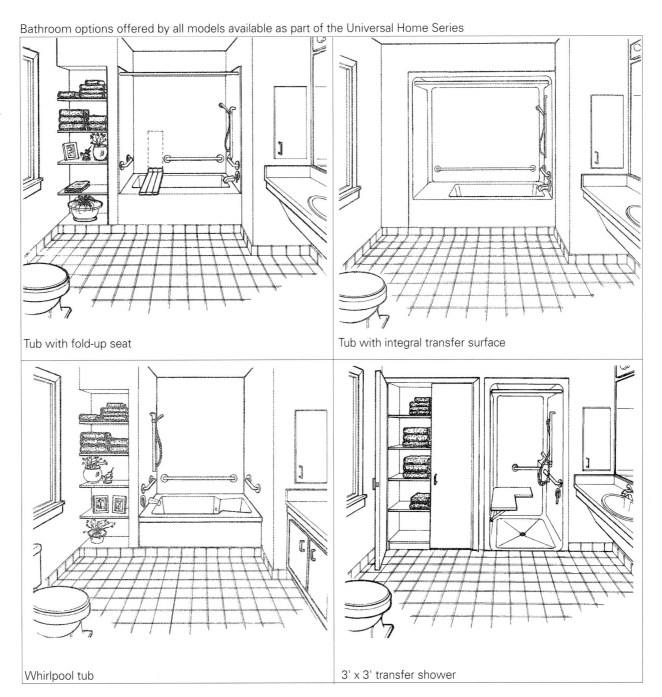

Bathroom options offered by all models available as part of the Universal Home Series

Tub with fold-up seat

Tub with integral transfer surface

Whirlpool tub

3' x 3' transfer shower

ROBINSON RESIDENCE

Architect
Universal Designers & Consultants, Inc.
Rockville, Maryland
Builder
Charles Wentz
Laurinburg, North Carolina

The Robinson residence is customized to address the homeowner's accessibility requirements. Since daily life requires the client to use a wheelchair, barrier-free design provides maximum access. The architect's long-standing involvement in making facilities accessible to people with disabilities enabled him to successfully meet his client's needs.

Because the Robinson residence is built entirely on grade, meandering paths provide access to the entrance. Raised planters and an accessible dock enable the homeowner to take full advantage of the amenities the lakeside site has to offer. The attached garage is large enough to accommodate a van and a second car. An efficiency apartment is incorporated above the garage should the need for assisted living arise.

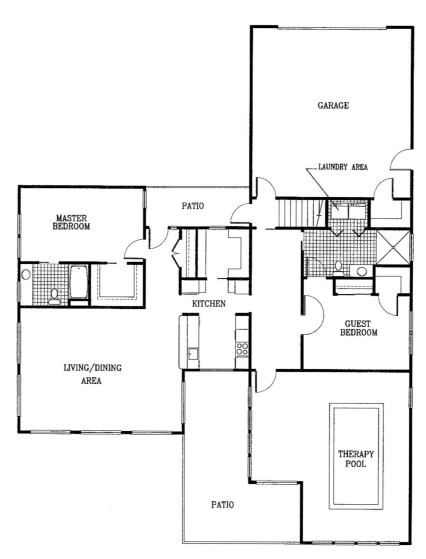

Floor plan of the Robinson residence

Inside, wide hallways and the open plan of the living/dining and kitchen areas ensure ample wheelchair maneuverability. The master bedroom is located adjacent to the front entry for emergency egress. Interior and exterior lighting controls are located beside the bed. A roll-in closet with an adjustable storage system is separated from the bedroom by a pocket door that allows unobstructed passage when open. The master bathroom features an accessible lavatory and an easy transfer tub.

In the kitchen, a large pantry/storage area is accessed through a pocket door that can be kept open and out of sight. Adjacent to another wide hallway is the guest bedroom, an indoor therapy-pool room and an accessible guest bathroom that doubles as a changing room. The bathroom features a roll-in shower and an accessible lavatory. The laundry area is designed as part of the guest bathroom.

Exterior views of the Robinson residence, oppo

A sidelight at the front door enables the homeowner to identify visitors. Low thresholds provide a smooth transition between interior and exterior. Slip-resistant tile and linoleum floors are used throughout the main circulation areas of the home. Lever hardware is provided on all doors. The lever handle on the master bedroom door is mounted within comfortable reach from a wheelchair.

The spacious living/dining area provides ample space for wheelchair maneuverability and versatility in furniture layout. Lake views are maximized through large casement windows with sills set at heights that allow viewing from a wheelchair or couch. The crank arm for the windows is located at the sill. Low sills also provide for emergency egress. A control center with communication, interior and exterior lighting and environmental controls is located near the couch.

Open plan of the living/dining area, below

Entry foyer, above

Roll-in shower in the guest bathroom, above

Guest bathroom showing the accessible lavatory, below

The master bathroom includes an accessible lavatory. Kneespace below the guest lavatory is also provided. The toilet and tub are positioned to allow easy transfer. Fold-down grab bars are installed. A roll-in shower is installed in the guest bathroom. An accessible laundry area is designed as part of the guest bathroom.

61

Kitchen view from the living/dining space

Kitchen view from the roll-in pantry

The kitchen is designed to maximize wheelchair accessibility. Counters, set at 34, 36 and 42 inches above the floor, have been installed to enable comfortable food preparation activities from a sitting or standing position. Counter space is provided on either side of the cooktop. The shallow sink allows easy placement or removal of dishes. The sink drain is offset to minimize plumbing in the kneespace area. The combination of instant hot water, soap dispenser, pull-out faucet, and lever controls adds to the homeowner's convenience in preparing for and cleaning up after meals. Counter space next to the wall oven allows for the placement of hot items. The large roll-in pantry includes adjustable shelving.

Wall oven with storage drawers below and a counter for placing hot items

Shallow sink with offset drain, pull out faucet, soap dispenser and instant hot water

Cooktop with kneespace below and counter space on either side

THE ADAPTABLE HOUSE

Designer
Living Design
Vancouver, Washington
Contractor
Pat M. Bridges and Associates
Tigard, Oregon

The Adaptable House featuring barrier-free design was showcased in the Portland Street of Dreams in 1988. This model home was sponsored by Northwest Natural Gas Company, the National Association of Home Builders and the Home Builders Association of Metro Portland. The design includes a variety of accessible features. The house is adapted for wheelchair users, those who are sight or hearing impaired, or who have mobility limitations. The Adaptable House welcomes everyone, of all ages, including young children and their grandparents.

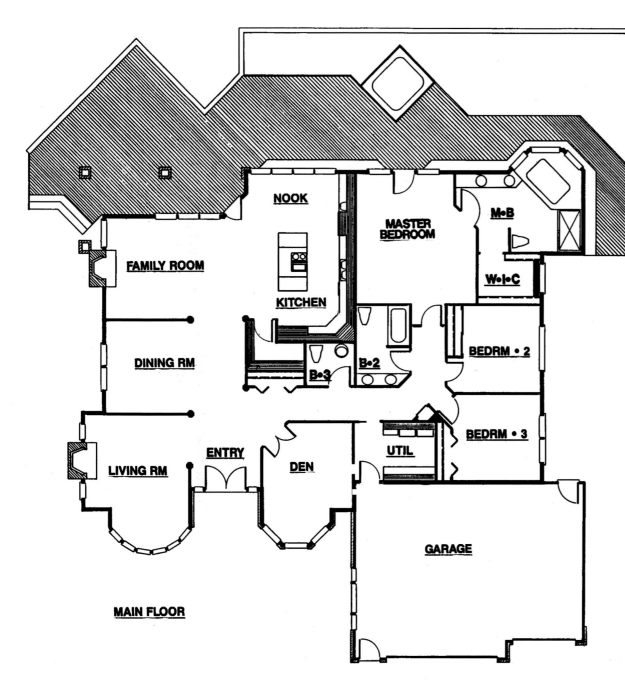

FAMILY ROOM

NOOK

KITCHEN

DINING RM

MASTER BEDROOM

M•B

W•C

BEDRM • 2

B•3

B•2

BEDRM • 3

ENTRY

LIVING RM

DEN

UTIL

GARAGE

MAIN FLOOR

The Adaptable House contains more than 2,800 square feet with a three-car garage, living room, family room, den, kitchen, three bedrooms and two-and-a-half baths. The plan has ample space in all rooms for easy wheelchair maneuvering.

All doorways are 34-inches wide to permit wheelchair access. Doors throughout are fitted with lever hardware for ease of operation. Electrical outlets are raised to within a comfortable reach area. The garage, with 8-foot-high double doors, will accommodate a van and two additional vehicles. A fully accessible deck can be reached from both the kitchen area and the master bedroom through no-step doorways.

Floor plan of the Adaptable House

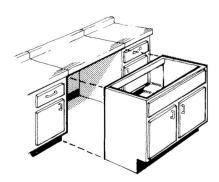
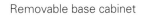

Removable base cabinet

Accessible desk or food prep

Accessible kitchen island

The top portion of the kitchen counter is independently supported, allowing it to remain in place if the cabinet is removed. The counter can be adjusted in height.

The desk has ample kneespace and can double as a food preparation area. This is further enhanced by the location of a lower level sink, just to the right of the desk.

The center island has a counter-height shelf with kneespace provided. The shelf can be used for food preparation or dining.

Pull-out tray can also be used as a food prep surface

Double bathroom sink

A microwave is placed within comfortable reach of someone in a seated position. A pull-out tray is next to the microwave to facilitate ' transferring food into and out of the oven.

A contrasting color strip along the edge of the vanity top is a cue for people with visual impairments. The base cabinets in the master bathroom are removable to provide kneespace. The tub has a transfer seat and easily reachable hot and cold water controls. In addition, a curbless shower with a hand-held shower head and seat has been installed. The blinds surrounding the tub area are controlled by a remote switch.

THE EXCELSIOR

Designer/Builder
Wick Building Systems, Inc.
Marshfield, Wisconsin

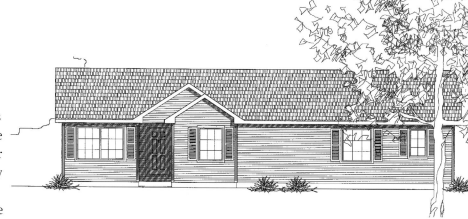

Wick Building Systems, Inc. (a large, 40-year-old Midwestern company with three factories in Wisconsin) specializes in the production of custom "factory-crafted" panelized and HUD code (manufactured) homes, and has made a commitment to build Universally Designed homes. Now in design development, the Excelsior (a HUD code home) is not yet in production, but it is intended to act as a catalyst to inspire a variety of custom floor plans that meet individual needs.

The purchaser may choose from a wide variety of barrier-free options available or may customize any design to meet individual needs. The goal of the options package is to enable purchasers to live independently in their own living environment. Wick is confident that its custom designs are affordable and take advantage of the most advanced building materials and construction practices.

Wick markets mostly to Wisconsin and surrounding states and its home packages are erected by Wick personnel. However, it could make its barrier-free HUD code model available virtually nationwide through its dealer networks. An increased level of quality control and cost savings through large-scale production are some of the advantages of its factory-crafted techniques. Wick believes its product compares in quality and is more affordable than a site-built equivalent. According to Wick, in an "apples-to-apples" comparison a conventionally constructed home would cost approximately 10 to 20 percent more than its factory-produced equivalent, depending on the dealer and location.

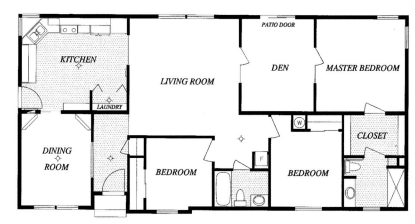

Floor plan of the Excelsior

Accessible kitchen layout

The laundry area

Kneespace is provided below the corner sink as well as below the adjacent counter. Counter heights can be customized for use in a seated position. Pull-out cutting board surfaces are available as an option. Accessible appliances such as the side-by-side refrigerator and front-control range are provided. The floor is finished with a slip-resistant material.

The home incorporates a laundry area designed as part of the large open kitchen. An adjustable ironing board can be used from either a sitting or standing position. Both washer and dryer are front loading. Ample storage has been provided.

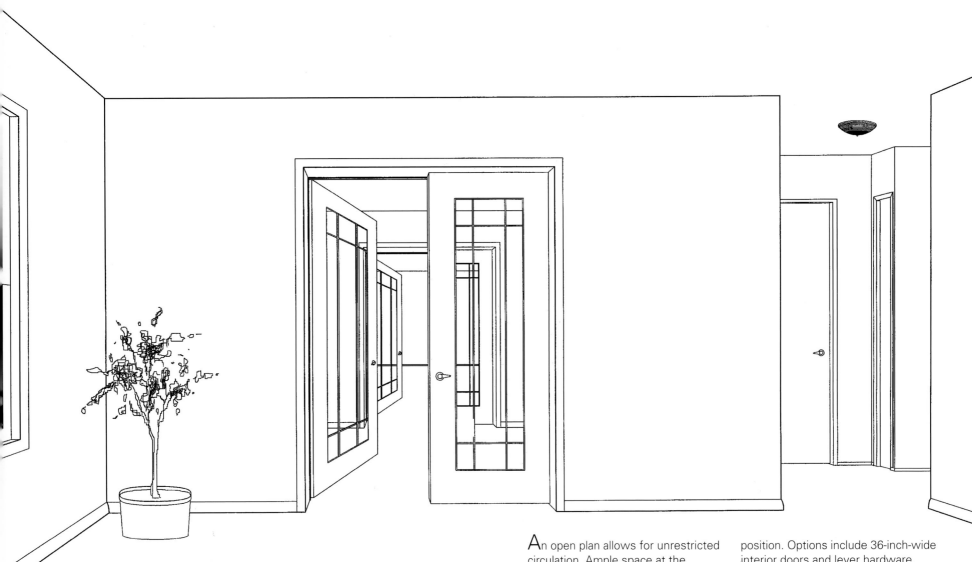

An open plan allows for unrestricted circulation. Ample space at the latch-side of doors facilitates easy approach and use of doors from a wheelchair. Double doors into the den add to the overall spaciousness and offer easy passage. Low window sill heights ensure full views from a seated position. Options include 36-inch-wide interior doors and lever hardware. Casement windows are also available as an option.

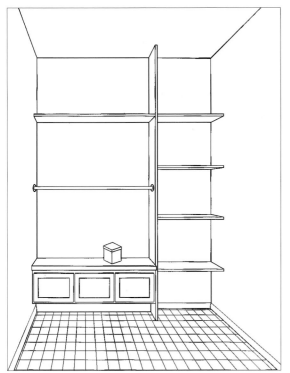

Accessible hanging poles and storage shelves

Roll-in shower with open-shelf storage

Accessible vanity and toilet area

The oversized closet in the master bedroom can be specified with a custom closet organizer systems to meet many differing needs. Lower height hanging poles and shelves, and low level storage bins can be included.

The master bathroom features kneespace below the sink and a separate toilet compartment outfitted with grab bars. The vanity height is lower than standard. As an option, a roll-in shower can be specified.

AN URBAN BARN

Architect
Winthrop Faulkner & Partners
Chevy Chase, Maryland
Contractor
The W™ P. Lipscomb Co., L.P.
Arlington, Virginia

This sophisticated addition to a small, compact home doubles the area of the original building. Sited on a large corner lot, the owners wanted to incorporate additional living and entertaining space with dramatic interior views, soaring two-story height and exposed structure. During the development of the project, the owner became partially disabled. The architects were then challenged to modify the design to adapt to the client's condition while retaining the desired character of the addition.

Exterior view of the addition showing the grass ramp that provides access to and from the garden area

In response to the owner's physical limitations, design modifications included adding ramps (one stone, one grass), providing maximum ¹/₂-inch-high thresholds, and sizing doorways and passageways to accommodate a wheelchair.

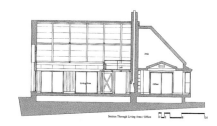

Section through living area/office

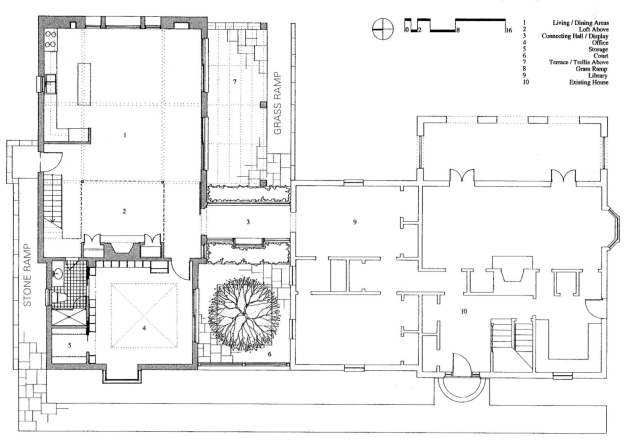

1	Living / Dining Areas
2	Loft Above
3	Connecting Hall / Display
4	Office
5	Storage
6	Court
7	Terrace / Trellis Above
8	Grass Ramp
9	Library
10	Existing House

Floor plan

Living area

Kitchen/dining area

The open plan of the barn-like home provides wheelchair accessibility with a minimum number of interior walls. Features in the living area include a remote-controlled gas fireplace and a slip-resistant floor finish.

Ample clear floor area and accessible work surfaces are provided in the kitchen. Windows throughout the space are low, allowing full views from a seated position. The casement windows are operable by means of a crank mechanism on the sill, within easy reach.

View of the transition space

A wide, glass hall connects the addition to the original building. The visual impact of this transition space is heightened by the small outdoor courtyard and stone terrace opening to the west and east.

A barn door installed on an overhead track requires no threshold and allows easy wheelchair passage into the addition. Floor-to-ceiling windows permit an unobstructed view from any height.

75

THE STAFFORD

Architect/Builder
Eid-Co Buildings, Inc.
Fargo, North Dakota

Eid-Co Buildings, Inc., is a medium-sized builder of affordable and energy-efficient housing units. The company believes that most purchasers in the target area of the Northern Great Plains do not require "exotic" or extensive changes to meet special needs. Most simply want "step-free" living, extra storage and a compact and efficient floor plan. The Stafford, which is available as both an attached and detached model, can be easily modified to meet the specific needs of buyers. Some Stafford models have been built with roll-in showers, bathtubs with lifts, and special computer/media equipment.

Aside from its Universal Design features, this home is a model of energy conservation. It includes super-insulated walls and ceilings, triple glazed maintenance-free windows, an insulated foundation, and an air-exchange system for moisture and air quality control.

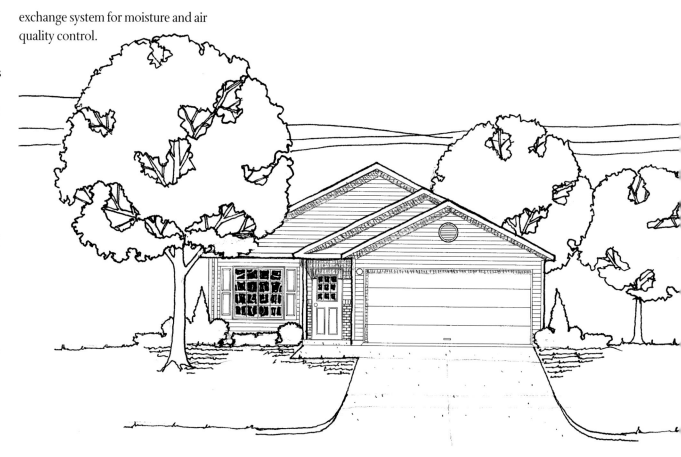

The detached version of the compact and efficiently planned Stafford model has a level front entry that opens into a slip-resistant foyer. Low-pile carpet and slip-resistant floors are specified throughout the home. Vaulted ceilings provide spacial interest. The large garage is van-accessible and includes an area for storage.

A "mud room" with laundry facilities off the garage provides ample maneuvering room and extra storage. The den that can double as a second bedroom has access to a patio. Both bathrooms are accessible. A roll-in shower is available as an option. The U-shaped kitchen contains ample clear floor area.

PATIO

DEN

MASTER BEDROOM

LINEN

LINEN

BATH

MSTR BATH

KITCHEN

REF

DW

W

D

DINING

STORAGE

LIVING

GARAGE

First floor plan

Exterior view of the Stafford

A level path connects the front entry to the garage, creating an accessible entrance into the home. Divided lights in the front door allow for visitor identification and additional light. The covered entryway affords protection from the elements.

Large living room windows add to the open feel of the home while admitting the sun's radiation, an advantage in the cold winters of the Great Northern Plains. The living area windows provide full views from a sitting or standing position.

Level path connects the garage with the front entry and the street

The kitchen has a U-shaped plan. The compact "work triangle" works well for people with limited mobility. The large peninsula is multi-functional; it can be used for family activities and crafts, food preparation, and casual entertaining. Sink-base and cooktop-base cabinets are removable for wheelchair access.

The milti-functional kitchen peninsula with the living and dining areas in view, above

Open plan of the Stafford, below

THE SUNRISE HOME

Architect
Arlo Braun and Associates, PC
Denver, Colorado
Builder
Johnson Communities of Nevada, Inc.
Las Vegas, Nevada

The Sunrise Home was introduced in 1994 in the Horizon View community of Las Vegas, Nevada. Typical of the upper-middle income homes in this largely seniors community, the Sunrise is designed to be fully wheelchair accessible.

The challenge for Johnson Communities of Nevada, Inc. (one of Denver's largest builders) was to produce a home with a design and spatial configuration that would appeal to the mass market, yet meet the unique, changing needs of people throughout their lifetime, all at an affordable price. Certain tradeoffs were required. Extensive market research revealed that the vast majority of people do not require a formal living room. As a result, the company eliminated the formal living area and added space to hallways and bedrooms, achieving a home with a sense of openness.

Floor plan of the Sunrise

Universal bathroom options

A gently sloped 4-foot-wide ramp makes the front entry accessible. The oversized van-accessible garage, with an 8-foot-high door, is equipped with an automatic door opener. An automatic self-opening and closing door from the garage to the house is also included.

Exterior view of the Sunrise, above

Rear view of the Sunrise, below

The rear view shows the accessible backyard patio. Thresholds are no more than 1/2 inch high.

The fully accessible bath features a large roll-in shower equipped with a seat that lifts up when not in use. Grab bars are installed completely around the shower. An anti-scald regulator is provided. The open vanity provides for roll-under sink access. The pocket door ensures unobstructed wheelchair turnaround space.

Wheelchair accessible bathroom option, above

Open kitchen plan, below

Sink-base cabinet doors are removable for wheelchair access. Counters of varying heights allow food preparation activities from either a standing or sitting position. A lower level desk area with wheelchair access provides additional work space. Upper level cabinets are installed lower than usual. A side-by-side refrigerator also increases access.

Dual bedroom suites make this home adaptable to the changing needs of any family. The first suite can be modified to be fully accessible. In addition, hardwired smoke alarms, a burglar alarm, front door bell and telephone bell are all connected to four-color strobe lights to alert people with hearing impairments. Closet poles are installed at a low height for accessibility.

Accessible master suite 1, above

Accessible master suite 2, below

The second bedroom suite is nearly identical to the first. The attached bath includes a dual sink, bathtub and compartmentalized water closet. Low windows increase views out. Electrical switches and outlets are within comfortable reach.

83

UNIVERSAL DESIGN FEATURES CHECKLIST AND GRAPHIC GUIDELINES

This checklist has been developed to help designers and builders perform a quick analysis of how well a home design incorporates universal design features. The checklist was developed by the Center for Universal Design, Center for Accessible Housing, at North Carolina State University, and is used here with permission. Other design information resources, listed on pages 104–117, also provide guidelines for accessible housing design, and these resources should be consulted and compared to the suggestions in this checklist.

The drawings provide guidance for architects and builders in designing and building accessible living environments. They suggest commonly accepted minimum and maximum dimensions for clearances and accessibility.

ENTRANCES

- Provide an accessible route to the entrance from vehicle drop-off area or parking.
- Maximum slope to the entry door should be 1:20.
- Provide a covered entryway, if possible, for shelter from the weather.
- Provide a 5-foot-square maneuvering space.
- Provide a package shelf or bench to hold parcels or groceries.
- Provide a full-length sidelight at the entry door (which allows occupants to see who is at the door before opening it, and also increases natural light in the foyer). .
- Use a movement-sensor light control to turn lights on and off.
- Provide ambient and focused lighting at the lockset to aid in operation.
- Use high-visibility address numbers on the facade that faces the road.

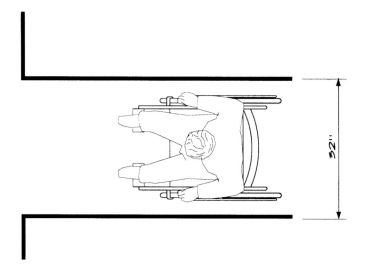

Minimum clearance for one wheelchair

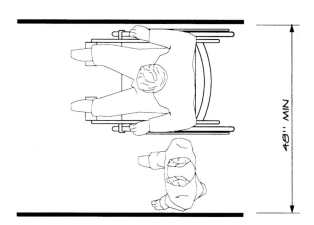

Minimum clearance for a wheelchair and ambulatory person

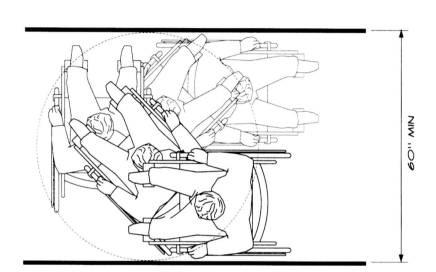

Minimum clearance needed to rotate a wheelchair

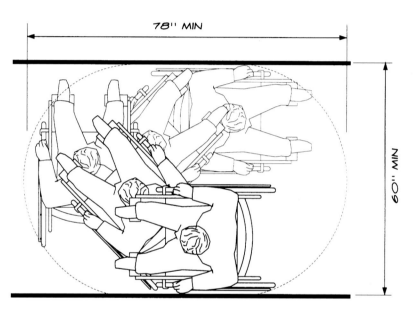

Minimum clearance needed for wheelchair U-turn

GENERAL HOME INTERIOR DESIGN

- Use lever-type door handles throughout.

- A force of no more than 5 pounds should be needed to operate and open doors.

- Use 32 inches minimum clearance for door opening widths throughout.

- Provide an 18-inch minimum space at the latch side of doors.

- Use flush thresholds or those that have no more than ½-inch rise.

- Provide adjustable height closet rods and shelves (which also increase storage space).

- Accessible routes throughout the home should be 42 inches wide, with a minimum of 32 inches for wheelchair clearance.

- Light switches should be no more than 44 inches to 48 inches above the floor (which also makes them accessible to children).

- Electrical outlets should be no more than 18 inches above the floor.

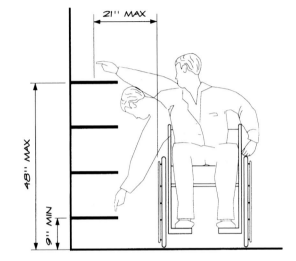

Maximum side reach over shelves

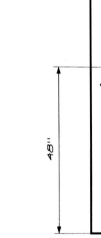

Maximum side reach in closets

- Windows for views should have sills no higher than 36 inches above the floor (which permits views for those seated and increases natural lighting).

- Crank-operated casement windows are a preferable style.

- Use loop handle pulls on all drawers and cabinets.

- Floors should have high-contrast, glare-free surfaces and trim.

- Provide a 5-foot-square maneuvering space in all rooms.

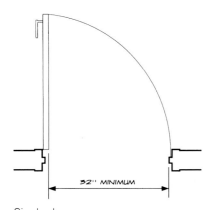

Single door

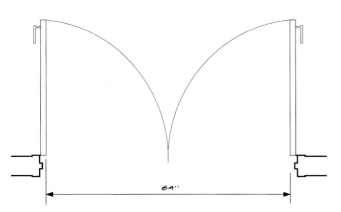

Double door

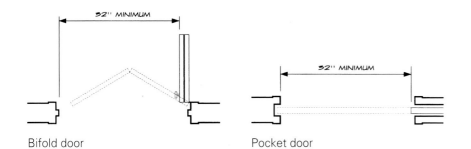

Bifold door   Pocket door

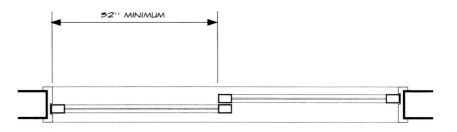

Sliding glass door

Transition strip

Threshold

Level change

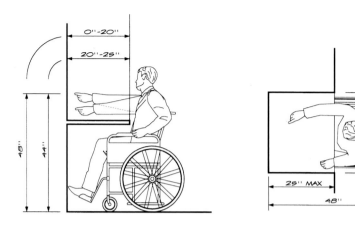

Maximum forward reach over an obstruction

KITCHEN DESIGN

- Use lever-type faucets for ease in adjusting temperature and volume.

- Provide kneespace under the sink and near the cooktop.

- Provide variable-height work surfaces between 28 inches and 45 inches above the floor (to permit everyone in the household to help with meal preparation).

- Use a contrasting color for border treatments at the edge of countertops.

- Provide stretches of continuous counterspace for sliding heavy objects.

- Pull-out drawers should extend fully to allow easy access.

- Provide pull-out shelves in base cabinets (making it easier to maneuver large items in and out).

- Use adjustable height shelves in wall cabinets.

- Provide full-height pantry cabinets with storage from top to bottom (to permit access from all heights, and to maximize storage).

- Provide a 30 inch-by-48 inch area of approach in front of all appliances.

- Use appliances with front-mounted controls.

- Cooktops with staggered burners to eliminate dangerous reaching are preferable.

- Provide glare-free task lighting.

BATHROOM DESIGN

- Use lever-type faucets for ease in adjusting temperature and volume.

- Provide kneespace under lavatory.

- Lavatory counter height should be a minimum of 32 inches above the floor.

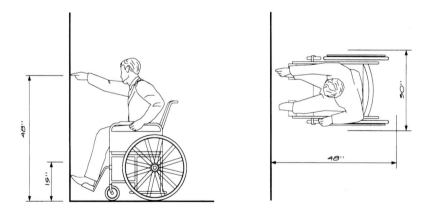

Forward reach limit

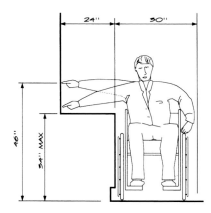

Maximum side reach over obstruction

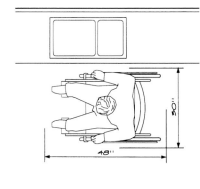

Parallel approach

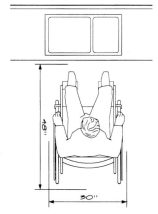

Front approach

- Extend mirror to lavatory back-splash to make it low enough for a wheelchair user and people of diminutive stature.

- Offset controls in tub or shower so that they can be operated from outside the fixture.

- Provide an integral transfer seat in the tub or shower.

- Use an adjustable height shower head.

- Provide grab-bar blocking and bars in the tub or shower (which can also be used for hanging towels).

- Use a mixer valve with pressure balancing and hot water governor (to prevent scalding and conserve hot water).

- Allow 18 inches of maneuvering space at both ends of the tub or shower.

- Center toilets at least 18 inches from sidewalls.

- Provide grab-bar blocking and bars around toilet (which can also be used for hanging towels).

- Provide a 30 inch-by-48 inch area of approach in front of all fixtures.

ENERGY-EFFICIENT DESIGN CHECKLIST

Designers and builders can work with the energy of the sun, natural light, ventilation, and the insulation of the earth to make houses more energy efficient. This can be accomplished through passive solar strategies, utilizing insulating glass, shading, orientation, thermal mass, and ventilation. As a result, mechanical systems can be smaller to compensate for some or all of the extra cost for a better house. In the long run, money will be saved through smaller energy bills, and a more comfortable house will result. This checklist should be used as a guide to help architects and builders to create more energy-efficient accessible housing.

SITING

- If the house plan is an elongated shape, position its long axis in the east-west direction.

- In cold and temperate climates place most windows toward the south, to gain solar heat. In hot climates place most windows toward the north, to protect from solar heat.

- Make use of natural slopes by berming the house into the ground, when these slopes do not block desirable views or desirable solar access. Berming protects from wind, reduces heat loss during the heating season, and reduces heat gain during the cooling season.

LANDSCAPING

- Plant evergreens to shield the house from cold winds (cold and temperate climates) or hot winds (usually hot and dry climates).

- Consider evergreens or deciduous trees with dense, long-lasting foliage to shade all windows for climates with year-round hot weather.

- With significant heating and cooling, plant deciduous trees to offer seasonal shading. Because the sun is low in the east and west, tree foliage should also be low, and the trees can be distant from the house. On the south side, however, the sun is high during summer, so tree foliage needs to be high for shading.

PASSIVE SOLAR DESIGN

In cold and temperate climates:

- Place most windows on the south side, fewest on the north side, to maximize solar gain and to reduce heat loss. The west elevation should not have many windows. Unless you have high cooling loads, east windows do not have a major affect on energy use.

- Use south-facing clerestories to bring the sun deeper into the house.

- Shade south-facing windows with overhangs, and east or west windows with deep porches or with vertical fins.

- Use thermal mass (brick, concrete, tiles, thick gypsum board) in rooms with large, south-facing windows to moderate and store solar heat. Earth berming averages the winter and summer temperatures in the rooms affected. If the earth-bermed room can be warmed in winter through south windows, this strategy will be successful.

- Except in high-humidity areas, natural ventilation is usually beneficial for extended periods of time. Enhance it by placing windows on opposite walls of the house. For houses with high spaces, place windows at the top. Do not encourage air infiltration during winter; specify tight-closing windows.

In locations such as southern California, where both the summer and winter are mild:

- Place most windows north and south. South windows allow solar gain during heating periods. Opposing north windows allow good cross-ventilation during cooling periods.

- Use south-facing clerestories with operable windows to bring sun and light deeper into the house and to ventilate. Ventilation can also be fan-assisted.

- Use thermal mass (brick, concrete, tiles, thick gypsum board) in rooms with solar exposure (most important south, but also east and west) to moderate and store solar heat. Earth berming can be successful, but is probably not cost-effective unless the terrain easily permits it, since the energy use in such climates is low.

- South-facing windows are well-shaded with overhangs, while east- and west-facing windows can be shaded by deep porches or by vertical fins.

- Facilitate natural ventilation by placing windows on opposite sides of the house, such as south and north, or low and high. If there are dominant breezes, place larger operable windows on the leeward side.

In hot and arid climates, such as Arizona and Nevada, with year-round high temperatures during the day and cool or cold nights:

- Place most windows on the south side, some on the north side, and few if any on the west side. East windows can help heat recovery from cold nights, if the glass area is not excessive and creates overheating.

- Use south-facing clerestories to bring sun and light deep into the house.

- Shade south-facing windows with overhangs, and east and west windows with deep porches or vertical fins.

- Use thermal mass throughout the house, including exterior and interior walls and floors to moderate and store solar heat. Earth berming can also provide desirable, year-round cooling.

- Facilitate natural ventilation by placing windows on north and south sides and high and low parts of the house, such as at the top of a two-story space.

In hot and humid climates, such as southern Texas and Louisiana, with year-round high temperatures, small variations between day and night, and extended periods of high humidity:

- Place most windows to the north, fewer south, and as few as possible east and west.

- Shade south-facing windows with overhangs, and east and west windows with deep porches or vertical fins. Interior shading devices are of very little effectiveness.

- Thermal mass is effective in saving energy if it continually cools the house. Earth berming is a good strategy because the ground several feet below the surface remains at a constant temperature. Brick, block, or tile may not be effective unless they are in contact with the ground.

ENERGY-EFFICIENT CONSTRUCTION

In cold and temperate climates:

- In wood-frame construction, create a well-insulated, tight shell with 2x6 framing and R-19 insulation. Or use 2x4 framing with R-13 insulation with exterior insulating sheathing.

- In wood-frame construction, use exterior air retarders (also called air barriers) that are vapor permeable to protect from air intrusion.

- In wood-frame construction, use a vapor retarder inside, unless engineering calculations show otherwise.

- In steel-frame construction, which has significant thermal bridging, use sheath framing with insulation on the exterior side.

- Consider using structural insulated panels—rigid insulation between two rigid sheets of plywood or pressed wood—a very effective insulation system, since there is no thermal bridging. In cold climates use at least R-15 insulation, R-20 if cost-effective.

- Consider using log construction for storing solar heat gains. This construction performs as well as walls with higher R-value. Performance is best in sunny climates.

- If the attic has joists, insulate between and above the joists with blanket, blown, and sprayed insulation. If the attic has trusses, insulate between them with a blanket. Insulate above the truss bottom chord to prevent air from leaking around the insulation between trusses. Above-chord insulation should be blown or sprayed.

- Provide perimeter insulation for the slab.

- For unconditioned basements insulate the floor above. If conditioned, insulate outside the walls when waterproofing is applied.

- Insulate pipes, especially if they are located in unconditioned spaces.

- Use insulating (double-pane) windows with low-e glass for solar gain and ventilation.

- If you use thermal mass, insulate it from contact with the ground.

- Use efficient lighting. Use T-8 triphosphor fluorescent lamps with electronic ballasts in kitchens and bathrooms. Triphosphor fluorescent lamps have very good color rendition and are energy frugal (70 to 85 percent savings compared to conventional incandescent lamps).

- Use compact fluorescent lamps in such areas as bedrooms and living rooms to save 60 to 75 percent in electricity costs over conventional incandescent lamps.

- Use electronic ballasts to save additional energy (25 to 40 percent over conventional magnetic ballasts) and reduce noise.

- Use efficient appliances. Look for the Department of Energy-published energy ratings and choose one with a low number.

- Use heating systems with 80 to 90 percent combustion efficiency. Gas, oil, and propane are the conventional fuel sources. Save energy with programmable and multiple thermostats.

- Electric should be used for resistance heating, and heat pumps for combustion equipment. Choose systems with heating seasonal performance fraction (HSPF) ratings of at least 6; ratings of 9 are available. Save energy with programmable and multiple thermostats.

- Consider using geothermal heat pumps, which draw cooling and heating from the ground through vertical holes drilled into the ground, or a horizontal pipe loop under the yard. Cost is double or triple of air-to-air, but energy efficiency is also triple in heating and about double in cooling. Can be cost-effective even in very cold climates because ground temperature is constant. Choose systems with seasonal energy efficiency ratings (SEER) greater than 16.

- Use efficient domestic hot water (DHW) systems. Eighty percent efficiency is common, with up to 95 percent available.

In hot and arid climates, such as Arizona and Nevada, proceed the same as for cold and temperate construction strategies above.

In mild climates, such as southern California:

- Fill all shell cavities with insulation and use relatively airtight construction to ensure comfort.

- Use windows for solar gain and ventilation.

- Use efficient lighting (see above), since in addition to direct energy savings, it may be possible to eliminate significant cooling loads.

- Use efficient appliances (see above).

- Consider using air-to-air heat pumps, which are cost-effective for heating and cooling where electricity cost is not very high; choose units with SEER of more than 10. Usually not cost-effective in very cold climates.

- Use efficient DHW systems (see above).

In hot and humid climates:

- Create a well-insulated, tight shell.

- In frame construction, use vapor retarders on the outside of the wall. Do not use vapor retarders in climates with hot and humid periods, and that require some heating, since moisture can come from either inside or outside the house. Let the walls breathe.

- Shade all windows.

- Facilitate contact of any thermal mass with the ground.

- Use efficient lighting and appliances (see above).

- Use efficient DHW systems (see above).

- Use efficient air-conditioners, either through-the-wall or split systems, with SEER of 8 to 12. Save energy with programmable and multiple thermostats.

SUSTAINABLE DESIGN CHECKLIST

This checklist is provided to guide designers and builders in the development and construction of houses that are sustainable, have lower environmental impact, improve the health and well-being of their occupants, and conserve natural resources. The checklist touches upon a wide range of issues, from site-planning considerations through selection criteria for construction materials. Energy-conservation measures, which are an important aspect of Sustainable Design, are discussed in the previous checklist.

SITE PLANNING

- If possible, help the client select a site with access to mass transportation, pedestrian and bike paths, and nearby services.

- If possible, help the client select a site with short connections to existing utilities and infrastructure. This results in less disruption of the site, and often results in significant cost savings.

- Protect natural site features such as rock out-croppings, trees, and shrubs to prevent soil erosion. Recycle trees and bushes that are taken down as mulch.

- Use earth berms, hills, and swales to control and minimize site water runoff. Consider providing a retention pond to hold water on-site, and to provide irrigation water for landscaping.

- Include a composting/recycling area on-site, easily accessible from the house.

LANDSCAPING

- Use low-maintenance, drought-resistant plants, shrubs, and ground cover to reduce water consumption.

- Avoid the use of chemical fertilizers and pesticides on lawns and landscaping elements. Native plant species often require little or none of these treatments.

- Avoid landscaping materials that leach pollutants into soils, groundwater, or nearby streams. For example, creosote or CCA-treated landscaping ties can be replaced with non-treated woods or with newer, less toxic pressure-treated timbers.

- Use reclaimed water (from retention ponds or cisterns, for example) for landscape irrigation.

BUILDING MATERIALS AND PRODUCTS

Building materials and products affect the environment in a variety of ways, ranging from the impact of their production (energy use, pollution), to their durability, to their impact as waste at the end of their useful life. Assessing building materials over this range of environmental considerations is called "cradle-to cradle" life-cycle assessment. These assessment criteria can assist in selecting materials with lower environmental impacts.

- Choose durable materials that will last longer, even if they cost a bit more. Life-cycle costs are often lower for more durable products, as maintenance and replacement costs are reduced.

- Use materials with low "embodied energy" in their production and transport. Embodied energy is that required to manufacture a product from its raw materials into its finished form, and to transport the products to the building site. Low embodied-energy materials include products made from natural resources (such as wood or stone), products that require minimal processing, and products that are locally produced (to minimize transportation).

- Choose materials and products with recycled or reconstituted content (such as engineered wood, insulation made from recycled newspaper, or recycled glass tiles). Look for recycled materials with a high "post-consumer" content.

- Where possible, choose materials that can be easily recycled at the end of their useful life.

- For materials that are not easily recyclable, look for those that are biodegradable, or those classified as non-hazardous waste.

- Avoid products containing chlorofluorocarbons (CFCs) or hydrochlorofluorocarbons (HCFCs), where possible. CFCs, which have been banned from most products in the United States, are responsible for ozone-depletion in the earth's upper atmosphere. HCFCs, while much less harmful than CFCs, still deplete ozone and are scheduled for phase-out within the next 20

years. Some types of rigid foam insulation boards, typically extruded polystyrenes, use HCFCs in their production. HCFCs are also used as refrigerants in many air-conditioners and heat pumps.

- Look for independent certification of a material's or product's environmental characteristics. Organizations such as Scientific Certification Services (SCS) or Greenseal evaluate various construction products and provide certification "seals" of the product's environmental benefits.

INDOOR AIR QUALITY

- Select materials and furnishings with low volatile organic compound (VOC) off-gassing. Paints, sealers, adhesives, carpets, and engineered wood are products often associated with off-gassing. Lower-emitting formulations of most of these products are readily available.

- Use a mechanical ventilation system to assure adequate fresh air, especially in "tight" energy-efficient houses.

- Install a carbon monoxide alarm to warn against harmful concentrations of this poisonous combustion by-product gas.

- In areas of the country where radon is common, provide adequate ventilation to avoid harmful concentrations of this poisonous gas.

WATER CONSERVATION

- Use infrared sensors or automatic shut-off faucets at sinks.

- Use low-flush toilets.

- Use low-flow aerators on shower heads and faucets.

- Use low water consumption appliances, including dishwashers and washing machines.

CONSTRUCTION AND DEMOLITION PRACTICES

- Salvage existing materials and products, where possible, if the work involves remodeling or demolition. Many communities have construction product resalers who refurbish and resell items ranging from heavy timbers to lighting fixtures, doors, and hardware.

- Separate construction and demolition debris to allow for reuse or recycling of valuable materials, particularly metals and wood. In many areas, the costs for separating these items can be more than offset by selling the scrap material and through reduced tipping fees at landfills.

ACCESSIBLE BUILDING PRODUCTS AND EQUIPMENT

This directory to accessible products, equipment, and specialties for residential use will help architects, designers, and builders in specifying items designed to aid people with disabilities. The Association for Safe and Accessible Products (ASAP) promotes the development and use of such products by producing a quarterly "Special Interest Forum" on specific design issues or product lines, and by participating in research. You can contact ASAP at: 1511 K Street, NW, Suite 600, Washington, DC 20005, 202-347-8200.

DIVISION 8: DOORS AND WINDOWS

08360: Garage Doors

Clopay Building Products Co.
312 Walnut Street
Suite 1600
Cincinnati, OH 45202-4036
800-225-6729
(van-accessible doors)

08710: Accessible Door Hardware

Dor-O-Matic
Architectural Hardware Division
7350 West Wilson Avenue
Harwood Heights, IL 60656-4786
800-543-4635
(motorized door openers)

Extend, Inc.
P.O. Box 864
Moorhead, MN 56561-0864
(lever/knob converter)

HEWI, Inc.
2851 Old Tree Drive
Lancaster, PA 17603
717-293-1313
(lever hardware)

Kwikset Corp.
516 East Santa Ana Street
Anaheim, CA 92803-4250
714-535-8111
(lever hardware)

Lindustries, Inc.
21 Shady Hill Road
Weston, MA 02193
617-237-8177
(lever/knob converter)

Marks USA
5300 New Horizons Blvd.
Amityville, NY 11701
1-800-526-0233
(level hardware and door closers)

Meroni Locks of America, Inc.
2121 W. 60th Street
Hialeah, FL 33016
800-749-5625
(push-type locksets)

Power Access Corp.
Bridge Street
P.O. Box 235
Collinsville, CT 06022
800-344-0088
(motorized door openers)

Schlage Lock Co.
2401 Bayshore Blvd.
San Francisco, CA 94134
415-467-1100
(lever hardware, easy-grip keys)

Titon, Inc.
P.O. Box 6164
South Bend, IN 46660
219-271-9699
(push-button locksets)

Weiser Lock Co.
6660 Weiser Lock Drive
Tucson, AZ 85746
800-677-LOCK
(lever hardware, easy-grip keys,
deadbolts)

Yale Security, Inc.
PO Box 25288
Charlotte, NC 28229-8010
800-438-1951
(level hardware and door closers)

08730: Weatherstripping and Thresholds

Andersen Windows, Inc.
100 Fourth Avenue North
Bayport, MN 55003-1096
612-439-5150
(ramped patio door sill insert)

National Guard Products
540 North Parkway
PO Box 70343
Memphis, TN 38107
800-647-7874
 (low profile metal thresholds)

Pemko
P.O. Box 3780
Ventura, CA 93006
800-283-9988
(low profile metal thresholds)

Weather Shield Windows and Doors
Medford, WI 54451
800-477-6808
(low profile metal thresholds)

08760: Window Hardware and Specialties

Andersen Windows, Inc.
100 Fourth Avenue North
Bayport, MN 55003-1096
612-439-5150
(lever hardware, lock actuators,
motorized openers)

Pella Corp.
102 Main Street
Pella, IA 50219
800-84-PELLA
(lever hardware, lock actuators)

Truth Hardware
700 West Bridge Street
Owatonna, MN 55060
800-866-7884
(motorized window openers)

Weather Shield Windows and Doors
Medford, WI 54451
800-477-6808
(lock actuators)

Window Ease
A-Solution, Inc.
1332 Lobo Place, NE
Albuquerque, NM 87106
505-256-0115
(actuators for sliding windows)

DIVISION 10: SPECIALTIES

10300: Fireplace Specialties

Heat-N-Glo
6665 West Highway 13
Minneapolis, MN 55378
800-669-HEAT
(remote-control fireplaces)

10800: Toilet and Bath Accessories

Arjo
8130 Lehigh Avenue
Morton Grove, IL 60053
800-323-1245
(bathtub transfer seats)

Beneke
Sanderson Plumbing Products, Inc.
P.O. Box 1367
Columbus, MS 39703-1367
800-647-1042; 800-356-1524 (in state)
(elevated toilet seats, grab bars)

Bobrick Washroom Equipment, Inc.
11611 Hart Street
North Hollywood, CA 91605-5882
818-764-1000
(shower seats)

Franklin Brass
P.O. Box 4887
Carson, CA 90749-4887
800-421-3375
(grab bars, bathtub and shower
seats, elevated toilet seats)

Hafele
P.O. Box 4000
Archdale, NC 20263
910-889-2322
(toilet and bath accessories)

Handi-Move
Accessibility Design
2933 Dakota Avenue South
Minneapolis, MN 55416
612-925-0301
(transfer device)

HEWI, Inc.
2851 Old Tree Drive
Lancaster, PA 17603
717-293-1313
(grab bars, bathtub and shower
seats, adjustable mirrors)

HITEC Group International, Inc.
8205 Cass Avenue, Suite 109
Darien, IL 60559
800-288-8303
(grab bars, bathtub and shower
seats, elevated toilet seats)

Linido USA
1090 McCallie Avenue
Chattanooga, TN 37404
800-698-4504
(grab bars)

Pressalit Products
P.O. Box 6820
Piscataway, NJ 08855
800-217-1929, ext. 1000
(padded supports, transfer seats,
adjustable supports)

Seachrome Corp.
9819 Klingerman Street
South El Monte, CA 91733
800-955-2476
(grab bars)

Silcraft Corp.
528 Hughes Drive
Traverse City, MI 49686
800-678-7100
(bathtub and shower transfer seats)

SureHands
Accessibility Design
2933 Dakota Avenue South
Minneapolis, MN 55416
612-925-0301
(transfer device)

DIVISION 11: EQUIPMENT

11455: Kitchen and Bath Cabinets

Aristokraft
P.O. Box 420
Jasper, IN 47547
812-482-2527
(accessible kitchen and bath cabinets)

The Kiwi Connection
82 Shelburne Center Road
Shelburne, MA 01370
413-625-9506
(accessible cabinet hardware)

Kraftmaid Cabinetry, Inc.
16052 Industrial Parkway
Middlefield, OH 44062
216-632-5333
(accessible cabinets)

Merillat Industries
Amera-Division
1 Merrillat Court
Loudonville, OH 44842
419-994-5571
(accessible cabinets)

Norcraft Companies, Inc.
30 E. Plato Boulevard
St. Paul, MN 55107
612-297-0061
(accessible kitchen cabinets)

Yorktowne Cabinets
Yorktowne, Inc.
P.O. Box 231
Red Lion, PA 17356
717-244-4011
(accessible kitchen cabinets)

11452: Residential Appliances

Amana Refrigeration, Inc.
Amana, IA 52204
800-843-0304
(refrigerators and stoves)

Asko
903 N. Bowser, Suite 200
Richardson, TX 75081
800-367-2444
(washers, dryers, dishwashers)

Equator Corp.
Arena Tower II
7324 Southwest Freeway, Suite 855
Houston, TX 77074
800-935-1565
(all-in-one washer/dryer)

Frigidaire Corp.
6000 Perimeter Drive
Dublin, OH 43017
800-685-6005
(refrigerators, washers, dryers, dishwashers, ranges)

GE Appliances
Appliance Park
Louisville, KY 40225
502-452-3071
(refrigerators, washers, dryers, dishwashers, ranges)

Jenn-Aire Magic Chef
3035 Shadeland
Indianapolis, IN 46226
317-545-2271
(ranges)

Kenmore
Sears Merchandise Group
3333 Beverly Road
Hoffman Estates, IL 60179
708-286-7627
(refrigerators, washers, dryers, dishwashers, ranges)

Maytag
One Dependability Square
Newton, IA 59298
515-792-7000
(washers, dryers)

Whirlpool Corp.
2000 M-53, MD 4300
Benton Harbor, MI 49085-2692
(refrigerators, washers, dryers, dishwashers, microwaves)

11460: Unit Kitchens

Cervitor Kitchens Inc.
10775 Lower Azusa Road
El Monte, CA 91731-1351
800-523-2666
(compact kitchen units, under-
counter refrigerators)

DIVISION 12: FURNISHINGS

12535: Motorized Hardware—
Blinds, Shades, Draperies

Makita USA, Inc.
14930 Northam St.
La Mirada, CA 90638-5753
800-4-MAKITA
(automatic drapery openers)

DIVISION 14: CONVEYING
SYSTEMS

14235: Residential Elevators

Access Industries, Inc.
Elevator Products
4001 East 138th Street
Grandview, MO 64030-2837
800-825-1220
(residential elevators)

Cemco Lift, Inc.
P.O. Box 368
5191 Stump Road
Plumsteadville, PA 18949
800-726-7380
(residential elevators)

Concord Elevator, Inc.
107 Alfred Kuehne Boulevard
Brampton, ON, Canada L6T 4K3
800-661-5112
(residential elevators)

Flinchbaugh
390 Eberts Lane
York, PA 17403
800-326-2418
(wheelchair lifts, stair climbs)

Florlift of New Jersey, Inc.
41 Lawrence Street
East Orange, NJ 07017
800-752-LIFT
(residential elevators)

Otis Elevator Co.
1 Farms Springs
Farmington, CT 06032
800-441-OTIS
(residential elevators)

Robertson Custom Elevators
Olympic Tower
300 Pearl Street, Suite 200
Buffalo, NY 14202
716-842-4502
(residential elevators)

Whirlteq
208 McAleese Lane
Moncton, NB, Canada, E1A 3L9
800-298-1480
(residential elevators, wheelchair lifts)

DIVISION 15: MECHANICAL

15440: Plumbing Fixtures

Aqua Bath Co., Inc.
921B Cherokee Avenue
Nashville, TN 37207
615-227-0017
(accessible shower enclosures)

Aqua Glass Corp.
P.O. Box 412
Industrial Park
Adamsville, TN 38310
800-238-3940
(accessible bathtubs, showers,
wheelchair receptors)

American Standard
P.O. Box 6820
Piscataway, NJ 08855-6820
908-980-3000
(accessible toilets, sinks)

Braun Corp.
1014 S. Monticello
P.O. Box 310
Winamac, IN 46996
800-843-5438
(accessible showers)

Clarion Fiberglass
Star Route Box 20
Marble, PA 16334
814-782-3011
(accessible showers)

Concept Fiberglass, Inc.
1515 East 4th Street
P.O. Box 518
Grand Island, NE 68802
800-262-3559
(accessible showers)

Crane Plumbing
1235 Hartrey Avenue
Evanston, IL 60202
708-864-9777
(accessible bathtubs, showers,
wheelchair receptors, toilets, sinks)

Eljer Industries
P.O. Box 879001
Dallas, TX 75287-9001
800-435-5372
(raised toilets)

Fiat
255 Hutchings Street
Winnipeg, MAN, Canada R2X 2R4
204-633-6122
(accessible bathtubs and showers)

Great Lakes Plastics
501 W. Lawson Avenue
St. Paul, MN 55117
612-487-4897
(accessible shower enclosures)

International Cushioned Products
202-8360 Bridgeport Road
Richmond, BC, Canada V6X 3C7
604-244-7638
(soft bathtubs)

Kindred
1000 Kindred Road
Midland, Ontario, Canada L4R 4K9
800-465-5586
(shallow kitchen sinks)

Kohler Co.
Kohler, WI 53044
414-457-4441
(accessible toilets, sinks, showers,
bathtubs, shallow kitchen sinks,
sensor-activated faucets)

Lasco Bathware
3255 East Miraloma Avenue
Anaheim, CA 92806
800-877-0464
(accessible bathtubs, showers,
wheelchair receptors)

Ludibet USA, Inc.
1980 S. Quebec Street, Suite 4
Denver, CO 80231-3234
800-582-4338
(accessible toilets)

Moen, Inc.
25300 Al Moen Drive
North Olmsted, OH 44070-8022
800-321-8809
(accessible bathtubs, showers,
wheelchair receptors, sinks, faucets)

E.L. Mustee & Sons, Inc.
5431 West 164th Street
Cleveland, OH 44142
216-267-3100
(accessible bathtubs, wheelchair
receptors)

National Fiber Glass Products
5 Greenwood Avenue
Romeoville, IL 60441-1398
708-257-3300
(accessible bathtubs and showers)

Silcraft Corp.
528 Hughes Drive
Traverse City, MI 49686
800-678-7100
(accessible bathtubs and showers)

Sterling Plumbing Group, Inc.
2900 Gold Road
Rolling Meadows, IL 60008
708-734-1777
(shallow kitchen sinks, accessible bathtubs and enclosures, accessible faucets)

Tub-Master Corp.
413 Virginia Drive
Orlando, FL 32803
407-898-2881
(accessible showers and enclosures)

Universal-Rundle Corp.
217 N. Mill Street
New Castle, PA 16103
800-955-0316
(accessible showers and toilets)

Upper Tub
242 Northwood Drive
Yellow Springs, OH 45387
513-767-8181
(accessible bathtubs)

Urinette, Inc.
7012 Pine Forest Road
Pensacola, FL 32526
904-944-9779
(accessible toilets)

Warm Rain
P.O. Box 600
Houghton County Airpark
Hancock, MI 49930
906-482-3750
(accessible showers)

15445: Fittings, Trim, and Accessories

Cambridge Brass
140 Orion Place
Cambridge, ON, Canada N1R 5V1
800-724-3906
(sensor-activated faucets)

Chicago Faucet Co.
2100 South Clearwater Drive
Des Plains, IL 60018
708-803-5000
(accessible faucets, off-set drain pipes)

Delta Faucet Co.
55 East 111th Street
Indianapolis, IN 46280
317-848-1812
(accessible faucets)

Franke, Inc.
Kitchen Systems Division
212 Church Road
North Wales, PA 19454
800-626-5771
(accessible faucets)

Grohe America
900 Lively Boulevard
Wood Dale, IL 60191
800-323-9660
(accessible faucets)

Plumberex Specialty Products, Inc.
3188 Date Palm Drive, Suite 196
Cathedral City, CA 92234
800-475-8629
(anti-scald plumbing shields)

Rohl Corp.
1559 Sunland Lane
Costa Mesa, CA 92626
800-777-9762
(accessible faucets)

Speakman
P.O. Box 191
Wilmington, DE 19899-0191
302-764-9100
(motion-activated faucets)

World Dryer
5700 McDermott Drive
Berkeley, IL 60163
800-323-0701
(motion-activated faucets)

15950: Thermostats

Honeywell
1985 Douglas Drive North
Golden Valley, MN 55422-3992
800-345-6770, ext. 7175
(easy-to-read thermostat controls)

DIVISION 16: ELECTRICAL

16724: Signaling Devices

Duartek, Inc.
Fifty/Sixty Six Plaza
11150 Main Street, Suite 105
Fairfax, VA 22020
703-352-2285
(strobe smoke detectors)

Honeywell
1766 Old Meadow Lane
McLean, VA 22102
703-749-2065
(intelligent house control systems)

Interface Security Systems, Inc.
10646 Gulfdale, Suite 4
San Antonio, TX 78216
210-349-8864
(security and emergency systems)

Leviton
59-25 Little Neck Parkway
Little Neck, NY 11362
718-631-6579
(intelligent house control systems)

Mastervoice
10523 Humbolt Street
Los Alamitos, CA 90720
800-735-6278
(voice-activated controls)

NuTone
P.O. Box 1580
Cincinnati, OH 45201-1580
513-527-5100
(visual door signal)

UNIVERSAL DESIGN INFORMATION RESOURCES

There is a wealth of information for architects, designers, and builders on the design of accessible housing. The following sections list many of the resources available.

BOOKS AND ARTICLES

Abrahms, A. J. And M. A. Abrahms, *The First Whole Rehab Catalog: A Comprehensive Guide to Products and Services for the Physically Disadvantaged,* 1991.

"Accessible Products: Aids to Universal Design," *Interior Design,* v. 63, no. 11 (August 1992):102-7.

"The Adaptable Home," *Woman's Day Home Ideas,* Summer 1989.

Adaptable Housing, U.S. Department of Housing and Urban Development, 1987.

AIA Foundation, *Design for Aging: An Architect's Guide,* Washington, D.C.: The AIA Press,1985.

Alvarez, March, "Healthy Building," *Rodale's Practical Homeowner,* February 1987.

American Association of Retired Persons, Ronald Mace and Ruth Hall Phillips, *ECHO Housing: Recommended Construction and Installation Standards,* 1984.

American Association of Retired Persons, *Housing Options for Older Americans,* Washington, D.C., 1984.

American Association of Retired Persons and ITT Hartford, *The Hartford House —A Home for a Lifetime,* 1994.

American Association of Retired Persons, *The Perfect Fit: Creative Ideas for a Safe and Livable Home,* 1991.

American Association of Retired Persons, *Your Home, Your Choice: A Workbook for Older People and Their Families,* Washington, D.C., 1991.

American Foundation for the Blind, *Aging and Vision,* 1987.

American Institute of Architects and American Association of Homes and Services for the Aging, *Design for Aging: 1992 Review,* Washington, D.C., 1992.

American Institute of Architects and American Association of Homes and Services for the Aging, *Design for Aging: 1994 Review,* Washington, D.C., 1994.

American National Standards Institute, *American National Standard for Accessible and Usable Buildings,* Falls Church, VA.

Amundson, R., "Disability, Handicap, and the Environment," *Journal of Social Philosophy,* v. 23, no. 1 (1992): 105-17.

Anders, Robert, and Daniel Fechtner, Universal Design Primer, Brooklyn, NY: Pratt Institute Department of Industrial Design, 1992.

Arthur, Paul, and Romedi Passini, *Wayfinding: People, Signs and Architecture,* New York: McGraw-Hill, 1992.

Barrier-Free Environments, Inc., *The Accessible Housing Design File,* New York: Van Nostrand Reinhold, 1991.

Barrier-Free Environments, Inc., *Adaptable Housing: Marketable Accessible Housing for Everyone,* U.S. Department of Housing and Urban Development, 1987.

Barrier-Free Environments, Inc., *Adaptable Housing: A Technical Manual for Implementing Adaptable Dwelling Unit Specifications,* U.S. Department of Housing and Urban Development, 1987.

Barrier-Free Environments, Inc., *UFAS Retrofit Guide,* Van Nostrand Reinhold, 1993.

Barrier-Free Plans, *Professional Builder and Remodeler Magazine,* 1991 House Plans Issue, 1991.

Beall, George Thomas, *Housing Older Persons in Rural America: A Handbook on Congregate Housing,* Washington, D.C.: International Center for Social Gerontology, 1981.

Beasley, Kim, "Home Sweet Home," *Paraplegia News,* Special Section, v. 48, no. 9, September 1994.

Bednar, Michael, *Barrier-Free Environments,* Stroudsburg, PA: Dowden Hutchinson, and Ross, 1977.

————, *Adaptable Marketable Housing for Everyone,* Washington, D.C.: U.S. Department of Housing and Urban Development, 1987.

Behar, Susan, "A Design Solution for 'Aging in Place,'" *The ASID Report,* January/February, 1991.

————, *The Human Lifespan: Growing Up/Growing Older.* Position paper presented at "Universal Design: Access to Daily Living" conference, Pratt University, May 1992.

————, "Universal Design Blends Function with Form," *Group Practice Journal,* July/August 1991.

Best, Don, "Creating Homes to Last a Lifetime," *Home Magazine,* February 1993.

Better Homes and Gardens Remodeling Ideas, *The Accessible Home: Remodeling Concerns for the Disabled,* Fall 1981.

Boston, Helen S., *Housing and Living Arrangements for the Elderly,* Washington, D.C.: National Council on the Aging, 1985.

Branson, Gary, *The Complete Guide to Barrier-Free Housing,* White Hall, VA: Betterway Publications, Inc., 1991.

"Build Barrier Free Baths for Everyone," *House Beautiful Kitchens and Baths,* Fall 1992.

"Building the Most Comfortable House for One-Level Living," *American Homestyle,* February/March 1995.

Burkart, Mary, "Accessibility = Profitability," *Qualified Remodeler,* v. 20, no. 2, February 1994.

Butler, Gayle, "Ideas for Your Bath," *Better Homes and Gardens Kitchen and Bath Ideas,* Summer 1989.

Carley, Christopher, "There Really Is No Place Like Home," *Qualified Remodeler,* v. 20, no. 2, February 1994.

Carlin, Vivian, *Can Mom Live Alone?* Lexington, MA: Lexington Books, 1991.

Carlin, Vivian, and Ruth Mansberg, *Where Can Mom Live?* Lexington, MA: Lexington Books, 1987.

Carstens, D. Y., *Site Planning and Design for the Elderly: Issues, Guidelines, and Alternatives,* New York: Van Nostrand Reinhold, 1985.

Cary, Jane Randolph, *How to Create Interiors for the Disabled: A Guidebook for Family and Friends,* New York: Pantheon Books (Random House), 1978.

"A Celebration of Disability Culture," *The Disability Rag and Resource,* September/October1995.

Center for Accessible Housing, *Definitions: Accessible, Adaptable, and Universal Design* (Fact Sheet), North Carolina State University, 1991.

————, *Financing Home Accessibility Modifications,* North Carolina State University, 1993.

————, *Housing Accessibility for Individuals with Visual Impairment or Blindness,* North Carolina State University, 1992.

————, *Universal Design of Decks, Porches, Patios, and Balconies,* North Carolina State University, 1992.

Center for Accessible Housing and North Carolina Cooperative Extension Services, North Carolina State University, *Accessible Stock House Plans Catalog,* 1993.

The Center for Universal Design, "Emerging Technologies for Independent Living: Technical Article," Raleigh, NC: University of North Carolina, 1995.

Champagne, J. R., and Satya Brink, *Designing Homes for the Aged,* Ottowa: National Research Council Canada, 1985.

Cheever, Ellen M., Marylee McDonald, Nick Geragi, and Annette DePaepe, *Kitchen Industry Technical Manual, Volume 3, Kitchen Equipment and Materials,* National Kitchen and Bath Association and University of Illinois Small Homes Council, 1993.

Cheever, Ellen M., Marylee McDonald, and Nick Geragi, *Bathroom Industry Technical Manual, Volume 3, Bathroom Equipment and Materials,* 1992.

Cheever, Ellen M., Marylee McDonald, and Nick Geragi, *Bathroom Industry Technical Manual, Volume 4, Bathroom Planning Standards and Safety Criteria,* 1992.

Cheever, Raymond, and Betty Garee, *An Accessible Home of Your Own,* Cheever Publishing, Inc., 1990.

Christenson, Margaret A., *Aging in the Designed Environment,* Binghamton, NY: The Haworth Press, 1990.

Cohen, Edie Lee, "Graceful Living," *Interior Design,* August 1992.

Cohen, Uriel, *Mainstreaming the Handicapped, A Design Guide,* Milwaukee, WI: Center of Architecture and Urban Planning Research, School of Architecture and Urban Planning, University of Wisconsin-Milwaukee, 1981.

Cohen, Uriel, and Gerald D. Weisman, *Holding on to Home: Designing Environments for People with Dementia,* Baltimore, MD: The Johns Hopkins University Press, 1991.

Connell, Bettye R., and Jon A. Sanford, "Individualizing Home Modification: Recommendations to Facilitate Performance of Routine Activities," in *Housing Adaptations to Accommodate Changing Needs: Research, Policy and Programs,* J. Hyde and S. Landsbury, eds., Newton, MA: Butterworth Press, 1997.

A Consumer's Guide to Home Adaptation, Adaptable Environments Center for the Massachusetts Housing Partnership, 1989.

Coombs, Amy, "Modifying Your Home in Dollars and Sense," *Arthritis Today,* November/December 1992.

Corbet, Barry, "What's So Funny About Disability?" *New Mobility,* February/March 1993.

Cosby, Robert L., and Teri Flynn, eds., *Housing for Older Adults: Options and Answers,* 1984.

Crosbie, Michael J., "Universal Hardware," *Architecture,* July 1991, pp. 88–89.

Cullinan, Gould, Irvine, Silver, "Visual Disability and Home Lighting," *Lancet,* 1979.

Cullinan, T. R., "Visual Disability and Home Lighting," *Journal of Rehabilitation Research,* 1980.

Danford, G. Scott, and Edward Steinfeld, "In Search of Methods for Measuring Enabling Environments," in *Measuring Enabling Environments,* Steinfeld and Scott, eds., New York: Plenum, 1992.

———, "Environmental Design: Enabling Technology of an Aging Society," in *Technology Innovation for an Aging Society,* Gloria M. Gutman and J. Watzke, eds. forth-coming.

DeJong, G., and R. Lifchez, "Physical Disability and Public Policy," *Scientific American,* June 1983.

Denno, Sandra, Brian A. Isle, Ginny Ju, et al., *Human Factors Design Guidelines for the Elderly and People with Disabilities,* Minneapolis, MN, 1992.

Department of Community Health, *Maintaining Seniors' Independence: A Guide to Home Adaptions,* Montreal General Hospital, 1989.

Design for Aging Resource Package, Aging Design Research Program, Washington, DC: American Institute for Architectural Research, 1996.

"Design Ideas for Special Needs," *Better Homes and Gardens Kitchen and Bath Ideas,* Summer 1985.

"Designs for Barrier-Free Kitchens," *Woman's Day Home Ideas,* Summer 1989.

DeSpain, J. J., "Home Modification: Balancing Accessibility, Beauty and Cost," *New Mobility,* v. 5, no. 18, November/December 1994.

Dickman, Irving R., Making Life More *Liveable: Simple Adaptations for the Homes of the Blind and Visually Impaired Older People,* American Foundation for the Blind, 1983.

DisabledUSA, Special Issue, December 1987.

Eastern Paralyzed Veterans Association, *Wheelchair House Designs.*

Federal Register, Volume 56, No. 144, *Final Fair Housing Accessibility Guidelines,* 1991.

Fisher, Thomas, "Enabling the Disabled," *Progressive Architecture,* July 1985, pp. 119–126.

Flanagan, Barbara, "A Manifesto for Change," *Metropolis,* May 1995.

Frechette, Leon A., *Accessible Housing,* McGraw-Hill, 1996.

Gaunt, L., "Can Children Play at Home?" in *Innovation in Play Environments,* P. F. Wilkinson, ed., London: Croom Helm, 1980.

General Electric, *Real Life Design,* Louisville, KY: GE Appliances, 1995.

Godwin, Phillip, "Homes Without Barriers," *Changing Times,* March 1988.

Golant, Stephen M., *Housing America's Elderly: Many Possibilities/Few Choices,* Newbury Park, CA: SAGE Publications, 1992.

Goldenberg, Leon, AIA, *Housing for the Elderly: New Trends in Europe,* New York: Garland STPM Press, 1981.

Goldsmith, S., *Designing for the Disabled* (3rd ed., fully revised), London: RIBA Publications, 1984.

Greer, N. R., "The State of the Art of Design for Accessibility," *Architecture 76,* January 1987, pp. 58–60.

Gutman, Gloria M., and Norman K. Blackie, eds., *Aging in Place: Housing Adaptations and Options for Remaining in the Community,* Burnaby, British Columbia: The Gerontology Research Centre, Simon Fraser University, 1986.

————, *Housing the Very Old,* Burnaby, British Columbia: The Gerontology Research Centre, Simon Fraser University, 1988.

————, *Innovations in Housing and Living Arrangements for Seniors,* Burnaby, British Columbia: The Gerontology Research Centre, Simon Fraser University, 1985.

Habitat for Humanity Planbook, Habitat for Humanity International, 1993.

Hart, Leslie, "Design for Special Needs," *Kitchen and Bath Business,* December 1992.

Hertz, Sue, "The User-Friendly Home," *House Beautiful,* November 1992.

Hiatt, Lorraine, "The Color and Use of Color in Environments for Older People," *Nursing Homes,* 1980.

Hildreth, G. J., and C. D. Hoyt, "Children and Privacy: Implications for Parents and Teachers," *Journal of Home Economics,* Winter 1981.

Hoglund, J. David, *The Intangible Qualities of Housing: Privacy and Independence in Housing for the Elderly,* privately published, 1983.

"A Home for All Seasons," Better *Homes and Gardens Remodeling Ideas,* Fall 1989.

"Home Improvements," Special Section, *Paraplegia News,* v. 48, no. 11, November 1994.

"Home Modifications," *Technology and Disability,* issue edited by Edward Steinfeld, v. 2, no. 4, Fall 1993.

Howell, Sandra C., *Designing for Aging: Patterns of Use,* Cambridge, MA: MIT Press, 1980.

Hyatt, L. G., J. Brieff, J. Horwitz, and C. McQueen, *Uses of Self-Help in Compensating for Sensory Changes in Old Age* (Grant Report), New York: American Foundation for the Blind, 1982.

The Illustrated Directory of Handicapped Products, Lawrence, KS: Trio Publications, Inc., published annually.

"The Impact of New Technologies," *Helioscope: European Disability Magazine,* Spring 1996.

Inman, M., M. Boschetti, and J. Inman, "Design Criteria in the Study of the Sustainable Residential Setting for the Independent Older Adult," paper presented at Environmental Design Research Association, Annual Meeting, Boulder, CO, 1992.

Jacobson, Julie, "Really Accessible Housing: Future Home Automated for Any Personal Limitation," *Electronic House,* March/April 1995.

Jensema, Carl, *Specialized Audio, Visual and Tactile Alerting Devices for Deaf and Hard of Hearing People,* edited by Dorothy Smith, 1990.

Johnson, Mary, *People with Disabilities Explain It All to You,* Louisville, KY: Advocado Press, ed., 1992.

Johnson, Patricia M., "Creation of the Barrier-Free Interior," *A Positive Approach,* 1995.

Kearney, Deborah S., *The New ADA: Compliance and Costs,* Kingston, MA: R.S. Means, 1993.

Koontz, T. A., and C. V. Dagwell, *Residential Kitchen Design: A Research-Based Approach,* New York: Van Nostrand Reinhold, 1994.

Lanspery, Susan, and Joan Hyde, eds., *Staying Put: Adapting the Places Instead of the People,* Baywood Publishing, 1997.

Lebovich, William L., *Design for Dignity: Accessible Environments for People with Disabilities,* Florence, KY: Van Nostrand Reinhold, 1993.

Lehman, Betsy, "Making a House Livable for Elderly," *Boston Globe,* July 22, 1985.

Leibrock, Cynthia, and S. Behar, *Beautiful Barrier-Free: A Visual Guide to Accessibility,* New York: Van Nostrand Reinhold, 1993.

Lifchez, Raymond, and Barbara Winslow, *Design for Independent Living,* Berkeley, CA: University of California Press, 1979.

Lippert, Joan, "Homes That Help," *Homeowner,* October 1988.

Lisak, J., K. Culler, and M. Morgan, *The Safe Home Checkout: Easy Assessment, Simple Solutions,* 1991.

Long, Richard G., "Housing Design and Persons with Visual Impairment: Report of Focus-Group Discussions," *Journal of Visual Impairment and Blindness,* January/February 1995.

Lusher, Ruth Hall, "Designing for the Life Span," *The Construction Specifier,* February 1988, pp. 31–32.

———, "Handicapped Access Laws and Codes," in *Encyclopedia of Architecture: Design Engineering and Construction,* vol. 3, Wilkes and Packard, eds., New York: John Wiley and Sons, 1989, pp. 646–659.

Lusher, Ruth Hall, and Ron Mace, "Design for Physical and Mental Disabilities," in *Encyclopedia of Architecture: Design Engineering and Construction,* vol. 3, Wilkes and Packard, eds., New York: John Wiley and Sons, 1989, pp. 748–763.

Mace, R., G. Hardie, and J. Place, "Accessible Environments: Toward Universal Design," in *Design Intervention: Toward a More Humane Architecture,* Preiser, Vischer, and White, eds., New York: Van Nostrand Reinhold, 1991.

Mace, Ronald, *Universal Design: Housing for the Lifespan of All People,* U.S. Department of Housing and Urban Development, Washington, D.C., 1988.

Mace, Ronald L., Barrier-Free Environments, Inc., *The Accessible Housing Design File,* New York: Van Nostrand Reinhold, 1991.

————, "Accessible for All: Universal Design," *Interiors and Sources,* v. 8, no. 17, September/October 1991, pp. 28–31.

————, *Definitions: Accessible, Adaptable, and Universal Design,* Raleigh, NC: Center for Accessible Housing, North Carolina State University, 1992.

Maytag Kitchen Idea Center, *The Accommodating Kitchen: Accessibility with Substance...and Style,* Maytag, 1994.

Miller, Katie, and Elizabeth Hite, *Accessibilities for Everybody,* University of Kansas.

Moore, Gary T., Kathryn H. Simmons, and Marleen M. Sobczak, *Alternative Housing for Older Adults: A Typology,* Milwaukee, WI: Center of Architecture and Urban Planning Research, University of Wisconsin-Milwaukee, 1985.

Moore, Lois J., and Edward R. Ostrander, *In Support of Mobility: Kitchen Design for Older Adults,* Cornell University, 1992.

Moore, Robin, Susan Goltsman, and Daniel Iacofano, *Play for All Guidelines: Planning, Design, and Management of Outdoor Play Settings for All Children,* Berkeley, CA: MIG Communications, 1992.

————, "The Case for Universal Design," *Aging International,* March 1995, pp.19–23.

Mueller, James, "Toward Universal Design: An Ongoing Project on the Ergonomics of Disability," *American Rehabilitation,* Summer 1990.

Mullick, Abir, "Bathing Easy," TeamRehab Report, April 1994.

Myers, Phyllis, *Aging in Place: Strategies to Help the Elderly Stay in Revitalizing Neighborhoods,* Washington, DC: The Conservation Foundation, 1982.

NAHB Research Center, *The Housing Accessibility Information System (HAIS),* October 1990, rev. January 1991.

————, *The Directory of Accessible Building Products,* 1995.

NAHB Research Center and Barrier-Free Environments, Inc., for the U.S. Department of Housing and Urban Development, *Residential Remodeling and Universal Design: Making Homes More Comfortable and Accessible,* 1996.

Nathanson, Eric, *Housing Needs of the Rural Elderly and the Handicapped,* Washington, DC, U.S. Department of Housing and Urban Development, Office of Policy and Development Research, 1980.

National Easter Seal Society, *Easy Access Housing for Easier Living,* brochure, 1991.

National Information Center on Deafness, *Homes and Housing for Aged Deaf Persons,* Washington, DC: Gallaudet University, 1991.

Newcomer, Robert J., M. Powell Lawton, Thomas O. Byerts, AIA, eds., *Housing an Aging Society,* New York: Van Nostrand Reinhold, 1986.

New York State Rural Housing Coalition, Inc. "Designing Housing to Meet Special Needs," *Rural Delivery,* June 17, 1993.

Nissen, LuAnn, Ray Faulkner, and Sarah Faulkner, *Inside Today's Home,* Harcourt Brace College Publishers, 1992.

Nolan, William, and Joseph Boehm, "Forever Young," *Better Homes and Gardens,* October 1994.

Nordic Committee on Disability in cooperation with the World Rehabilitation Fund, Monograph No. 31, *The More We Do Together: Adapting the Environment for Children With Disabilities,* World Rehabilitation Fund, Inc., 1985.

North Carolina Department of Insurance, *Accessible Housing: A Manual on North Carolina's Building Code Requirements for Accessible Housing,* Raleigh, NC: North Carolina Dept. Of Insurance, Special Office for the Handicapped, 1980.

Novotne, Sharon, "Easy Living in a Remodeled Ranch," *Remodeling Ideas,* Spring 1995.

Null, Roberta L., "A Universal Kitchen Design for the Low-Vision Elderly," *Journal of Interior Design Education and Research,* 1987.

————, "Environmental Design for the Low-Vision Elderly," *Journal of Home Economics,* Fall 1988.

————, "Kitchens Designed for the Low-Vision Elderly," *Journal of Vision Rehabilitation,* v. 2, no. 4.

————, "Universal Design for the Elderly," *Housing and Society,* v. 16, no. 3, 1989.

Null, Roberta L., with K.F. Cherry, *Universal Design: Creative Solutions for ADA Compliance,* Belmont, CA: Professional Publications, Inc., 1996.

"On the Eve of Universal Design: Homes and Products that Meet Everyone's Special Needs," *Home,* October 1988, pp. 95–104.

Orleans, Peter, "Kitchens," *Access Information Bulletin,* National Center for a Barrier-Free Environment, 1980.

Paskin, Nancy, and Lisa-Ann Soucy-Maloney, *Whatever Works— Confident Living for People with Impaired Vision,* Lighthouse, Inc., 1992.

Peterson, Mary Jo, *Universal Kitchen Planning: Designs That Adapt to People,* Hackettstown, NJ: National Kitchen and Bath Association, 1995.

————, *Universal Bathroom Planning: Designs That Adapt to People,* Hackettstown, NJ: National Kitchen & Bath Association, 1996.

Pirkl, James, *Transgenerational Design: Products for an Aging Population,* Florence, KY: Van Nostrand Reinhold, 1994.

Preiser, Wolfgang F. E., Jacqueline C. Vischer, and Edward T. White, eds., *Design Intervention: Toward a More Humane Architecture,* New York: Van Nostrand Reinhold, 1991.

Prosper, Vera, *Housing Older New Yorkers: Design Features,* New York State Office for the Aging, Division of Housing and Community Renewal, 1990.

Pynoos, Jon, and Evelyn Cohen, *Home Safety Guide for Older People: Check It Out/Fix It Up,* Serif Press, 1990.

Pynoos, Jon, and Evelyn Cohen, *The Perfect Fit: Creative Ideas for a Safe & Livable Home,* American Association of Retired Persons, 1992.

Quarve-Peterson, Julee, *The Accessibility Book: A Building Code Summary and Products Directory,* Fourth Edition, Crystal, MN, 1989.

Raisch, Marsha A., "A Kitchen for All Seasons," *Better Homes and Gardens Kitchen and Bath Ideas,* Fall 1994.

Raschko, Bettyann Boetticher, *Housing Interiors for the Disabled and Elderly,* New York: Van Nostrand Reinhold, 1982.

Regnier, Victor, ed., *Housing the Aged,* New York: Elsevier Science Publishing Co., 1987.

Research and Training Center on Independent Living, University of Kansas, *Guidelines for Reporting and Writing About People with Disabilities,* National Institute of Disability and Rehabilitation Research, 1987.

Rickman, Lenny, *A Comprehensive Approach to Retrofitting Homes for a Lifetime,* NAHB Research Center, 1991.

Roper, James, "Accessible and Full of Ideas," in *American Homestyle,* February/March 1995.

Rosenberg, Robert, O.D., *Lighting and the Aging Eye,* Lighthouse Low Vision Services, 1994.

Salmen, John P.S., "The Differences Between Accessibility and Universal Design," *Universal Design Newsletter*, July 1994.

Salmen, John P.S., for the American Association of Retired Persons, *The Do-Able Renewable Home: Making Your Home Fit Your Needs,* 1988.

Salmen, John P.S., and Julee Quarve-Peterson, *The 1995 Accessible Building Product Guide,* New York: John Wiley & Sons, Inc., 1995.

Schumacher, T. L., and G. Cranz, "The Built Environment for the Elderly: A Planning and Design Study, Focusing on Independent Living for Elderly Tenants," Princeton, NJ: Princeton University, School of Architecture and Urban Planning, 1975.

Shea, Scott, and Edward Steinfeld, "Accessible Plumbing" (multimedia program), Buffalo: Center for Inclusive Design and Environmental Access (IDEA), State University of New York/Buffalo, 1995.

————, "Technical Report: Accessible Plumbing," Buffalo: Center for Inclusive Design and Environmental Access (IDEA), State University of New York/Buffalo, 1995.

Sit, Mary, "Home Sweet Home," *Exceptional Parent's Guide for Active Adults with Disabilities,* Spring 1992.

Smith, Bret, and Tin-Man Lau, *Definition and Articulation of Human Factors Problem Areas in Residential Living Environments for the Elderly,* Auburn, AL, 1989.

Smith, Eleanor, *Entryways: Creating Attractive, Inexpensive No-Step Entrances to Houses,* Concrete Change, 1991.

Snell, Heather, *The Accessible Home: Renovating for Your Disabled Child,* IS Five Press, 1983.

"Special Universal Design Report," *Metropolis: The Urban Magazine of Architecture and Design,* November 1992.

Stathem, Rosemary, Jean Korczak, and Philip Monaghan, *House Adaptations for People with Physical Disabilities: A Guidance Manual for Practitioners,* HMSO - London, 1988.

Steinfeld, Edward, "Adaptable Housing for Older People," in *Housing for the Aged: Satisfactions and Preferences,* V. Regnier and J. Pynoos, eds., New York: Elsevier, 1987.

————, "Designing for All People: Resources for Students and Educators," outline for a college course, 1990.

————, "Design for the Life Span of All People? Spotlight on Adaptable Housing," *Rehab Brief,* v. 10, no. 12, pp. 1–4.

Steinfeld, Edward, and G. Scott Danford, "Automated Doors: Toward Universal Design," *The Construction Specifier,* August 1994.

————, "Theory as a Basis for Research on Enabling Environments," in *Measuring Enabling Environments,* Steinfeld and Scott, eds., New York: Plenum, 1992.

Steinfeld, Edward, Marcia Feuerstein, et al., "Hands on Architecture," Buffalo: Adaptive Environments Laboratory, State University of New York/Buffalo, 1987.

Steinfeld, Edward and Abir Mullick, "Universal Design: the Case of the Hand." *Innovation,* Fall 1990.

Steinfeld, Edward, and Scott Shea, "Designing Accessible Environments" (computer-aided instruction course), Buffalo: Center on Assistive Technology and IDEA, State University of New York/Buffalo, 1995.

————, "Technical Report: Accessible Cabinetry," Buffalo: Center for Inclusive Design and Environmental Access (IDEA), State University of New York/Buffalo, 1995.

Steinfeld, Edward, Scott Shea, William Zannie, and Abir Mullick, "Fair Housing Means Universal Design" (videotape program and instructor's handbook), Buffalo: Center for Inclusive Design and Environmental Access (IDEA), State University of New York/Buffalo, 1996.

Steven Winter Associates, Inc., *Homes for Everyone: Universal Design Principles in Practice,* U.S. Department of Housing and Urban Development, Washington, D.C., 1996.

Steven Winter Associates, Inc., Tourbier & Walmsley, Inc., Edward Steinfeld, and Building Technology, Inc. for the U.S. Department of Housing and Urban Development, *Cost of Accessible Housing: An Analysis of the Estimated Cost of Compliance with the Fair Housing Accessibility Guidelines and ANSI A117.*

Stewart, Mark, for Century 21 and National Easter Seal Society, *Lifetime Homes,* 1991.

Struyk, Raymond J., and Beth J. Soldo, *Improving the Elderly's Housing: A Key to Preserving the Nation's Housing Stock and Neighborhoods,* Cambridge, MA: Ballinger Publishing Co., 1980.

Sweet's Accessible Building Products, New York: McGraw-Hill, 1996.

Tetlow, Karin, "Contrasting Colors," *Interiors,* September 1993.

Uniform Federal Accessibility Standards, Washington, D.C., General Services Administration, U.S. Department of Defense, U.S. Department of Housing and Urban Development, U.S. Postal Service, 1984.

"Universal Design," *American Homestyle,* November 1994.

"Universal Design," *The Disability Rag and Resource,* March/April.

"Universal Design," Special Issue, *Interior Design,* v. 63, no. 11, August 1992.

Urban Land Institute, *Housing for a Maturing Population,* Washington, D.C., 1983.

Valins, Martin, *Housing for Elderly People: A Guide for Architects, Interior Designers and Their Clients,* New York: Van Nostrand Reinhold, 1988.

Wasch, William K., *Home Planning for Your Later Years,* Beverly Cracom Publishers, 1996.

Weal, Francis, and Francesca Weal, *Housing for the Elderly: Options and Design,* New York: Nichols Publishing, 1988.

Welch, Polly, ed., *Strategies for Teaching Universal Design,* Boston: Adaptive Environments, 1995.

White, Betty Jo, Mary H. Yearns, Glenda Pifer, and Roberta Null, "Future Environments: Forecasts and Issues," *Journal of Home Economics,* Spring 1989.

White & Partners, AB, compilers, *Designing with Care: A Guide to Adaptation of the Built Environment for Disabled Persons,* New York: United Nations, 1983.

Wilkoff, William L., and Laura W. Abed, *Practicing Universal Design: An Interpretation of the ADA,* Florence, KY: Van Nostrand Reinhold, 1994.

Williams, Chuck, "A House Without Barriers," *Fine Homebuilding,* September 1992.

Williams, F., "The Future of Aging," *The Archive of Physical Medicine and Rehabilitation,* June 1987.

Wrightson, William, and Campbell Pope, *From Barrier-Free to Safe Environments: The New Zealand Experience,* World Rehabilitation Fund, Inc., 1989.

Wylde, Margaret, *Enabling Products II —A Sourcebook,* Hackettstown, NJ: National Kitchen and Bath Association, 1995.

Wylde, Margaret, Adrian Baron-Robins, and Sam Clark, *Building for a Lifetime: The Design and Construction of Fully Accessible Homes,* Newtown, CT: Taunton Press, 1994.

————, "Accessible Bathrooms," *Fine Building,* April/May 1994, no. 88.

Yepsen, Roger, "A Home for Life," *Practical Homeowner,* July/August 1987.

Zube, Ervin H., and Gary T. Moore, eds., *Advances in Environment, Behavior, and Design,* New York: Plenum Press, 1991.

RESEARCH CENTERS AND ORGANIZATIONS

Abledata, 8455 Colesville Road, Suite 935, Silver Spring, MD 20910, 800-227-0216

Accessible Designs - Adjustable Systems, Inc., 94 North Columbus Road, Athens, OH 45701, 614-593-5240

Adaptive Environments, 374
Congress Street, Suite 301,
Boston, MA 02210, 612-695-1225

Adaptive Environments Lab, School
of Architecture and Planning,
University of Buffalo, University of
Buffalo, 390 Hayes Hall, Buffalo,
NY 14214

American Association of Retired
Persons, 601 E Street, NW,
Washington, DC 20049,
202-434-2277

American Deafness and
Rehabilitation Association, P.O. Box
251554, Little Rock, AR 72225

American Foundation for the Blind,
11 Penn Plaza, Suite 300,
New York, NY 10001

American National Standards Institute
(ANSI), 1430 Broadway, New York,
NY 10018, 212-868-1220

Architectural and Transportation
Barriers Compliance Board, 1331 F
Street, NE, Suite 1000,
Washington, DC 20004,
800-872-2253

Association for Safe and Accessible
Products, 1511 K Street, NW, Suite
600, Washington, DC 20005,
202-347-8200

Barrier-Free Environments, Inc., P.O.
Box 30634, Raleigh, NC 27622,
919-782-7823

Center for Inclusive Design and
Environmental Access, School of
Architecture and Planning,
University of Buffalo, Buffalo,
NY 14214

Center for Universal Design, North
Carolina State Univerity, School of
Design, Box 8613, Raleigh, NC
27695-8613

Center for Inclusive Design and
Environmental Access, School of
Architecture and Planning,
University of Buffalo, Buffalo,
NY 14214-3087, 716-829-3485

Disabled American Veterans National
Service Headquarters, 807 Mains
Avenue, SW, Washington,
DC 20024, 202-554-3501

Disability Rights Education Defense
Fund, 1633 Q Street, NW, Suite
220, Washington, DC 20009,
202-986-0375

Eastern Paralyzed Veterans
Association, 7520 Astoria
Boulevard, Jackson Heights,
NY 11370-1178, 718-803-3782

Hartford House (The), Community
Affairs Department, ITT Hartford
Insurance Group, Hartford Plaza,
Hartford, CT 06115

Hear You Are, Inc., 4 Musconetcong
Avenue, Stanhope, NJ 07874,
201-347-7662

Independent Living Research
Utilization Project, 2323 S. Shepard
Street, Suite 1000, Houston,
TX 77019

Lifease, 2451 15th Street, NW, Suite
D, New Brighton, MN 55112,
612-636-6869

The Lighthouse, Inc., 111 East 59th
Street, New York, NY 10022,
212-821-9200

Maddock, Inc., Catalog for
Orthopedic and ADL Products,
800-443-4326

National Center for Disability
Services, 201 I.U. Willets Road,
Albertson, NY 11507, 516-747-5400

National Council on Independent Living, 2111 Wilson Boulevard, Suite 405, Arlington, VA 22201, 703-525-3406

National Eldercare Institute on Housing and Supportive Services, Andros Gerentology Center, USC, University Park, MC-0191, Los Angeles, CA 90089

National Institute on Disability and Rehabilitation Research, U.S. Department of Education, 400 Maryland Avenue, SW, Washington, DC 20202

National Rehabilitation Engineering Center on Aging, 515 Kimball Tower, University at Buffalo, Buffalo, NY 14214-3079

National Rehabilitation Information Center, 8455 Colesville Road, Suite 935, Silver Spring, MD 20910, 800-346-2742

North Carolina Assistive Technology Project, 1110 Havaho Drive, Suite 101, Raleigh, NC 27609-7322, 919-850-2787

ProMatura, 428 N. Lamar Boulevard, Oxford, MS 28655, 601-234-0158

Sammons 1994 Catalog for Orthopedic and ADL Products, Sammons, P.O. Box 5071, Bolingbrook, IL 60440, 800-323-5547

Trace Research and Development Center, 1500 Highland Avenue, Madison, WI 53705

Universal Designers and Consultants, Inc., 1700 Rockville Pike, Suite 110, Rockville, MD 20852, 301-770-7890

Volunteers for Medical Engineering, 2201 Argonne Drive, Baltimore, MD 21218, 410-243-7495

WORLD WIDE WEB SITES

http://sound.media.mit.edu/~dpwe/ AUDITORY/asamtgs/asa95wsh/ 2aAA/2aAA1.html Transcript of: "Meeting the Challenges of the Americans with Disabilities Act: ASA 129th Meeting, Washington, DC, May 30 to June 6, 1995.

gopher://valdor.cc.buffalo.edu: 70/00/.nairc/.abledata/.fact-sheets/.ramps.fs6 Article: "Able Data Fact Sheet: Ramps"

gopher://valdor.cc.buffalo.edu: 70/00/.nairc/.abledata/.fact-sheets/.recline.fs4 Article: "Able Data Fact Sheet: Reclining Bath Seats"

gopher://valdor.cc.buffalo.edu: 70/00/.nairc/.abledata/.fact-sheets/.lifts.fs7 Article: "Able Data Fact Sheet: Stair Lifts"

gopher://valdor.cc.buffalo.edu: 70/00/.nairc/.abledata/.fact-sheets/.bathlift.fs3 Article: "Able Data Fact Sheet: Bath Lifts"

http://www.missouri.edu/~reslf www/access.html Accessible Housing, The University of Missouri-Columbia

http://www.faa.gov/arp/NOTADV. HTM Architectural and Transportation Barriers Compliance Board, Americans With Disabilities Act Accessibility Guidelines for Buildings and Facilities, notice of intent to establish advisory committee

http://www.faa.gov/arp/S9.HTM Americans with Disabilities Act Accessibility Guidelines (ADAAG), Checklist for Buildings and Facilities

gopher://libra.wcupa.edu: 70/00/diane/.files/1409 Book: Cost of Accessible Housing: An Analysis of the Estimated Costs of Compliance with Fair Housing Guidelines, available through Diane Publishing.

gopher://psupena.psu.edu:70/0%2 4d%2028302433 Article: "Kitchen Modifications Help Farm Wife with Multiple Sclerosis"

http://indie.ca/naaw.sniph/ National Access Awareness Week

http://www.gsa.gov/coca/SB_ paper.htm Paper: "People with Disabilities and NII: Breaking Down Barriers, Building Choice" excerpted from a document, The Information Infrastructure: Reaching Society's Goals Report of the Information Infrastructure Task Force Committee on Applications and Technology, published by U.S. Department of Commerce.

gopher://psupena.psu.edu:70/0%2 4d%2028302985 Article: "Rural Disabled Face Housing Hardships"

http://www.mbnet.mb.ca/crm/ housing/tenten.html Ten Ten Sinclair Housing Inc. offers description and contact information for Accessible Housing Unit and Accessible Housing Database in Manitoba.

http://cad9.cadlab.umanitoba.ca/ UofM/CIBFD.html The Canadian Institute of Barrier-Free Design offers descriptions of three elements of the Institute: Technical Services Program, Educational Program, and Research Program. Site includes contact information for the CIBFD whose mission is to improve the accessibility of buildings.

http://www.eit.com/mailinglists /www.lists/wwwtalk.1994q3/ 1061.html Talk: July–September 1994: WWW, Mosiac, and Access for People with Disabilities

CREDITS

Schultz Residence

Architect
Bruce Corson, AIA
Corson Associates, Architects
Sebastopol, CA

Photographer
George O'Keefe

Universal Home

Architect
James Fahy Design
Rochester, NY

Builder
Whitney East, Inc.
Rochester, NY

Consultants
Accessibility Designs and
Management, Inc.
Rochester, NY

Rochester Rehabilitation Center
Rochester, NY

Kitchen Design
Jean Schanker
JS Design
Rochester, NY

Fieldcrest II

Designer
Miles Homes Services, Inc.
Minneapolis, MN

Project Director
Kim Flesner

Director of Community-Based
Housing
Phil Dommer

Builder
The Philip Stephen Companies
Minneapolis, MN
Greenville, SC

Consultants
The Philip Stephen Companies

Universal Designers & Consultants,
Inc.
Rockville, MD

Accessibility Design
Minneapolis, MN

Illustrator
Mark Englund

Independent Living Homes™

Contractor
Storn Construction
Atlantic Beach, FL

The Owens

Designer/Builder
Jean DeLaura, ASID
Design One
Lemont, Ill

Universal Design

Designers
Shirley Confino-Rehder, CID, Affiliate
AIA/AAF
Jose Soria
Shirley Confino Interiors
Norfolk, VA

Photographers
Gary Qualls
Joe Rehder Video

The Future Home

Contractor
Robert Cook
Valley Contractors, Inc.
Phoenix, MD

Fairland Manor

Developer
Maurice H. Berk
President
Fairland Manor Development
Corporation
Silver Spring, MD

Architect
D.R. Brasher, AIA
President
American City Building
Columbia, MD

Builder
Korth Companies, Inc.
Gaithersburg, MD

Sales
Jackie Simon
ERA Mimi Selig Homes, Inc.
Barrier-Free Living Environments
Rockville, MD

The Heritage Retirement Communities

Architect
Richardson, Nagy, Martin
Newport Beach, CA

Builder
US Home Corporation
Englewood, CO

Kitchen and Bath Consultant
Mary Jo Peterson, CKD, CBD, CHE
Mary Jo Peterson Design Consultants
Brookfield, CT

Universal Home Series

Manufacturer
Excel Homes, Inc.
Liverpool, PA

Designers
Excel Homes, Inc.

Ronald L. Mace, FAIA
Director, Center For Accessible
Housing
North Carolina State University

Timber Ridge T-Ranch

Manufacturer
Excel Homes, Inc.

Designer
The Home Store
Whately, MA
Charlton City, MA

Center For Accessible Housing

Builder
The Home Store

Universal Ranch

Manufacturer
Excel Homes, Inc.

Designers
Excel Homes, Inc.

Center For Accessible Housing

Builder
Custom Care Homes
Holland, PA

Robinson Residence

Architect
John P.S. Salmen, AIA
President
Universal Designers & Consultants, Inc.
Rockville, MD

Builder
Charles Wentz
Laurinburg, NC

The Adaptable House

Designer
Living Design
Vancouver, WA

Contractor
Pat M. Bridges and Associates
Tigard, OR

Interior Design
Kay Green Design and
Merchandising, Inc.
Orlando, FL

The Excelsior

Designer/Builder
Steven Saffell
Director of Product Development
Wick Building Systems, Inc.
Marshfield, WI

An Urban Barn

Architect
Robert K. Sherrill, AIA
Project Architect
Winthrop Faulkner & Partners
Chevy Chase, MD

Contractor
The W$^{\underline{m}}$ P. Lipscomb Co., L.P.
Arlington, VA

Photographer/Covershot
© 1995, John Caleb Schwartz
Inwood, WV

The Stafford

Architect/Builder
Eid-Co. Buildings, Inc.
Fargo, ND

The Sunrise

Architect
Arlo Braun and Associates, PC
Denver, CO

Builder
Johnson Communities of Nevada, Inc.
Las Vegas, NV

Interior Design
Carole Eichen Interiors, Inc.
Santa Ana, CA

Photography
Jeffrey Aron
Irvine, CA

About the Author

Steven Winter Associates, Inc., is one of America's leading architectural consulting firms, with offices in Norwalk, Connecticut, and Washington, D.C. Among SWA's areas of expertise are building systems technology, energy-efficient design and engineering, accessibility, innovative home-building technology, and sustainable design. The firm is the recipient of several awards in the field of architectural research.